OPENING
GAMBITS

OPENING GAMBITS

The First Session
of Psychotherapy

Peter S. Armstrong, Ph.D.

JASON ARONSON INC.
Northvale, New Jersey

This book was set in 11 pt. ITC Galliard by Alabama Book Composition of Deatsville, Alabama, and printed and bound by Book-mart Press, Inc. of North Bergen, New Jersey.

10 9 8 7 6 5 4 3 2 1

Library of Congress Cataloging-in-Publication Data

Armstrong, Peter S.
    Opening gambits : the first session of psychotherapy / by Peter S. Armstrong.
      p. cm.
    Includes index.
    ISBN: 978-0-7657-0241-8
    1. Psychoanalytic counseling. 2. Psychoanalysis. I. Title.
BF175.4.C68 .A76 1999
616.89'14 21—dc21
                                                           99–041431

Printed in the United States of America on acid-free paper. For information and catalog write to Jason Aronson Inc., 230 Livingston Street, Northvale, NJ 07647-1726, or visit our website: www.aronson.com

To Linda,

my partner in work and in life,

and most of all, my friend.

Contents

Acknowledgments   ix

Introduction   xi

1   The First-Session Experience   1

2   The Therapist's Stance   9

3   The Contract—First Negotiations   65

4   The Contract—Fees and Legal Issues   83

5   Assessment   123

6   Transition to the Opening Phase   179

7   The Phone Call   187

8   My First Session with a Patient   193

9   Special Cases   207

References   225

Index   229

Acknowledgments

In the tradition of many who have written about clinical technique, I first thank my patients. They have trained me with understanding, with assertiveness, with patience, and with impatience. I have learned much of what is contained in this book from these people who have let me enter into their private spaces.

I enthusiastically thank my Institute, my family of psychoanalytic colleagues, for the training I received and the identity I found with them. My supervisors worked with me through the first and many later sessions with my patients. Jim Bews, Ph.D., Mike Horowitz, Ph.D., Dan Paul, Ph.D., Gail Steger, Ph.D., and Judy Welles, Ph.D., may recognize some of their imprints on my work. Of course, so much of who I am as an analyst I attribute to my own analyst. The effect of our first session together is evident in this book.

Many of my colleagues have influenced some piece of this work. All endured my years of attention to first session ideas as I turned conversations again and again to the ideas related here. Some of those who offered particular stories, ideas, and comments, or who read parts of the manuscript are Ann Coffey, Ph.D., Mac Coffey, Ph.D., Mark Hassan, Ph.D., Alan Karbelnig, Ph.D., Linda Miller, Ph.D., Mac Pigman, Ph.D., and Joy Schary, Ph.D.

I am grateful to the many therapists who have consulted with me, braving the anxieties of showing their work to a supervisor and letting me look in on the ways they conducted first sessions. I thank them for their honesty and for examples I have selected from their work.

I must thank Judy Cohen, my editor, who has the skills of a therapist, managing the anxieties of new authors. Thanks to Sigrid Asmus, the copy editor, who quietly improved my writing and corrected my random use of commas with an obsessiveness I aspire to but fail to reach.

Finally, this book was Jay Aronson's idea. He surprised me in our first session on the phone by suggesting I take the ideas of a class I was teaching and write a book. He made the process sound much simpler than it has been, but such illusion made continuing the work possible. Jay's colleague, Arthur Kurzweil, long ago encouraged me to write. Though I did not begin at his suggestion, his message finally came through via Jay. Arthur has given me the unique encouragement of a longtime friend.

Peter S. Armstrong
March 2000

Introduction

The psychotherapist who chooses to treat patients in the context of an extended relationship will conduct relatively few first sessions. The first session for this therapist and the potential patient will be a crucial one. Yet after the relationship is long under way, both therapist and patient may come to forget that first meeting.

As seldom as a first session occurs, as often as it is forgotten, it is a critical moment in the course of any successful therapy. In the most practical sense, the first session is the time when the possibility of engaging a patient in treatment is at its height. The first session must be conducted in a way that will allow the interested patient the greatest chance of using the therapist's services. Even if consciously forgotten, the first session is not forgotten by the unconscious because it is the introduction to the therapy and the way therapy will proceed, and thus analogous to one's development in life and introduction to the world and world of objects. We pay great attention to the infant's beginnings of relationship with mother; lovers pay great attention to their first meeting, first date, and other firsts. This book is about paying attention to the first session of the unique relationship, psychotherapy.

Literature on the first session of psychotherapy is minimal. Few writers have let us see how they conduct a first session. Many experienced therapists with whom I talked could not concretely describe how they approached the first session. As they considered the question each did, of course, describe a personal plan. Much is written on the opening phase, on the extended assessments necessary over the early weeks and months of therapy, but this first meeting, the first face-to-face contact, has seldom been addressed at length.

Perhaps one reason the first session gets so little attention is that once we try to talk about it the discussion rapidly leads into all of the other aspects of psychotherapy; it is impossible to speak only of the first session. All of what occurs in therapy is foreshadowed in the first meeting.

I became interested in the first session during my psychoanalytic training. As I began to understand my technique and my analytic relationship with patients, I could see pathways that had been formed and how difficult they were to change later in the therapy. I am reminded of the words of a man who became a professor after a career as a farmer. He said, "When you drive down a country road, pick your rut carefully, because you will be in it for a long time." Long-term, analytically oriented therapy is like that, and the ruts we travel are chosen in the first session.

The new wave of health insurance and managed health care may have made the first session of psychotherapy more important because it will be one of only a few sessions with the patient. This has nothing to do with the subject of this book. In fact it probably has nothing to do with what many young therapists are interested in today. I believe many students are training to become psychotherapists so that they can understand the workings of the human mind and ultimately help individuals to find relief from emotional turmoil and suffering. This cannot happen in one or a few sessions of psychotherapy. In fact such relief, if it is to be lasting, cannot result from a few of anything. Change takes time, and I believe it occurs in an adequate and rich human relationship with another person, the psychotherapist.

Given that we are in a time of lagging private practices and the undermining of psychotherapy by health-care insurers, marketers of quick fixes, and the promised cures of drugs, we ought to be very cognizant of the ways potential patients seek our services and what in our first meeting helps to engage them. Only a few are lucky enough to be actively sought out by an endless stream of patients. We must interest people in a service that has been maligned, poorly practiced, or undermined by some, yet that is still held in high esteem. The ability to conduct an effective first session is invaluable to the patient; it is also the foundation of an effective psychotherapy process and essential to a successful practice.

Opening gambits are the earliest moves of opponents to gain advantage in the complex and ancient game of chess. Freud (1913) used the metaphor of the chess game to explain the phases of psychoanalysis. The beginning and final moves of the chess game receive a great deal of attention; many books outline classic beginnings and endings. These moves can be categorized and summarized, learned and memorized. What occurs between them are more complex strategies that cannot be defined in an uncomplicated way. Psychoanalysis and psychotherapy must be started with some guidelines; this is what Freud tried to set out for the physicians of his day who were beginning to use his treatment. Most of the literature of psychotherapy is rightly focused on the "middle game" of psychotherapy, the interpretations, the therapeutic alliance, the day-to-day containment of a patient, and the theory that guides the work. But attention must also be paid to how we start and how this opening affects the continuation of a long-term analytic relationship. This is the subject of this book.

ASSUMPTIONS

This book is a study of the first session from the perspective of psychoanalytic theory and practice. I think of this in a broad sense, in keeping with Freud's (1914) assertion that any therapy that takes account of transference and resistance could call itself psychoanalysis. Analytic therapists come from a wide range of viewpoints, but many first-session issues are shared. The effect of transference is a key element of the first session. Transference has many different definitions and connotations, but I use it here to mean the phenomenon of a patient's attachment of meaning to the therapist's actions and words.

Psychotherapy takes time, even if not the extensive time of a formal psychoanalysis; it takes many sessions to accomplish its effects for the patient. Though contemporary society suggests that it ought to be quick, the development of a relationship is time-consuming. Quick romances or deep connections do not sound very authentic. Such experiences may be intense and emotionally stimulating, but do not offer the rich and involved relationship that can only occur over time. Many patients who seek psychotherapy may have never experienced that kind of connection. It requires genuine relationship in order to move forward, and that relationship is focused on the patient. If so focused, then the therapist's attention is directed to what will help the patient. The therapist's needs are secondary, although they are asserted as necessary within the relationship.

This focus on the patient is not meant to dismiss the therapist's needs. One of the goals of psychotherapy is the development of a mature sense of one's self as a separate individual. That will only occur for the patient if the therapist is personally cognizant of this and able to protect that separateness. Furthermore, psychotherapy is a business and the therapist's livelihood. This reality is a key issue in many transference feelings. Unfortunately the business of psychotherapy has been significantly complicated by recent managed health-care and third-party-payor changes. Legal demands on psychotherapists have further complicated the process of therapy and have invaded the privacy once considered essential for the treatment. It is my belief that a number of these changes have greatly damaged our ability to provide psychotherapy as the effective treatment it was developed to be; the fears therapists have of legal exposure can move their attention away from what was once the primary task, the patient's well-being and growth. I am writing at a time when the erosion of confidentiality is so great that the work of psychotherapy rests on shaky ground. Yet, day by day, hard-working, sincere psychotherapists continue to take on the task of providing a relationship, as confidential as they can make it, for patients seeking relief from suffering.

The work of psychotherapy is immensely demanding and requires a personal commitment from the therapist that extends beyond what is demanded in many other careers. It requires that the therapist become personally involved with the patient, containing the patient's anxieties and absorbing the patient's projections. The therapist must regularly attend to his own development. The work and its professional demands have been demeaned by the health-care system, by the public, and in the media. Even our profession has demeaned it by allowing what we do to be confused with all manner of other good experiences that people have, which are not in fact psychotherapy, the talking cure.

WHAT'S AHEAD

Four major topics will guide this exploration of the first session: (1) the therapist's stance, (2) the contract for psychotherapy, (3) the assessment for treatment, and (4) the transition to the opening phase of treatment. I have presented case material in a variety of ways. One fictional case, Gregg, runs through the entire book. He represents an amalgamation of my experiences with patients; he resembles everyone, but reveals no one. In addition, I have presented more traditional vignettes to illustrate certain ideas. I have taken a chapter to describe in detail just what I do in a first session. There is also a chapter on special cases, since we are most often not consulted by perfect patients, but individuals, who come to us in an infinite variety of ways. This book is not written as a literature review or research report, but is about the initiation of a treatment that is based in theory yet must be practiced as an art. To that end I suggest that each section be read as an essay about the issues, concerns, and challenges of the first session of psychotherapy.

The task of becoming a psychotherapist extends over one's entire career. We are always becoming, growing, integrating new experiences and ideas into our work, or else we are becoming less useful to the patients we try to help. It is a psychoanalytic ideal that the therapist is always in the process of self analysis. I have

cited and explained some of the important literature, but primarily I am writing about my integration of the literature, my
experience conducting psychotherapy, the many lessons patients
have taught me (some with patience, some not), my training,
supervision, personal analysis, and discussion with friends and
colleagues. You must do the same. I hope this book will be a part
of that process.

Chapter 1

The
First-Session
Experience

"I don't know what to talk about now that I've finally gotten to your office," Gregg says. These are his first words in his first session of psychotherapy, and in what may prove to be an extended relationship with this therapist. His anxiety is evident in the stiffness of his posture as he sits near the edge of my couch, alternately clenching and rubbing his hands together. I wait, not speaking, though his words seem to tug on me to respond in some way. I think back for a moment to our recent telephone conversation, remembering Gregg's request for a session, his indication that he had "never done this before" and that he was having "trouble in relationships." I scan this man that I have just met in person. He appears to be in his mid-thirties, he is dressed neatly in casual clothing; he could be attired for work, perhaps in his own business. His pause is long for social conversation, but given the unique circumstances of the therapy relationship, I let it continue. Gregg struggles to contain his anxiety and succeeds to the extent that he gathers his words and goes on to say, "Maybe I could begin by telling you a little about myself and why I called you. That will be a little easier to say first. . . ." As Gregg goes on, I wonder what will happen between us and what conflicts he will present to me. I am most concerned at this point that I listen and observe closely and act conservatively, so as not to disrupt or unnecessarily skew his conscious and unconscious presentation of himself. I imagine to myself that Gregg has been relatively successful in life according to standards of career and income, but that more privately he feels a sense of failure, loneliness, and hopelessness. He may now feel some hopefulness in having begun psychotherapy, but I realize he will yet experience the pain and hopelessness of his inner life as we begin to unravel who he is and who he might become.

BEGINNING, REPEATING, AND CHANGING

The first session of psychotherapy is a crucial moment for both the therapist and patient. For the therapist it is the moment when the possibility of change must be demonstrated; for the patient it is a moment in which the possibility of something new may be obstructed by the tendency to repeat. Beginnings contain the hope for something new and must be intertwined with an openness to the surprise of what cannot be predicted. Some writers of psychoanalytic technique tell us to be open to surprise, not lost in rigidity of technique that blinds us as therapists to what must be seen as new. Schafer (1983) highlights this as an analytic attitude; Ogden (1989) makes this idea the centerpiece of his chapter on beginning treatment.

Potential patients often express reluctance about psychotherapy because they perceive it as placing too much emphasis on the past. They want answers for the present and relief from their presently felt problems. This conception is of course a misunderstanding of how intensely focused psychotherapy is on the present and on beginning to see the world anew. A patient comes to a therapist because he wants to change his life, to stop feeling so afraid of choices, to become more effective at his career, or to find a passion where it seems no passion can be found. This can sound very motivated, but something has to be given up in order to meet these hopes for change. Something supports the experience that choices must be frightening, that the career cannot be enhanced, or that life must be passionless. Something supports these experiences from deep inside the new patient, who tenaciously holds on to the familiar in spite of the conscious hope to change.

Beginnings contain a remnant of the old, something that must be left behind in order for the new experience to occur. Marrying ends the aloneness and freedoms of singleness; entering a career ends the comforts and dependencies of being a student; divorcing ends the secure familiarities of marriage and the pain of a stagnant relationship; moving to a new town involves leaving friends and places known for new places and new explorations. Psychotherapy begins with a wish to end the limitations of one's present way of living, often without cognizance of the comforts of that familiar way of living. As exciting as beginnings are, the implicit end of something familiar also stirs reluctance to make the change. At an actual beginning we experience our reluctance to end something in anxieties and ambivalence that are not so noticeable when the beginning is just a fantasy. For the psychotherapy patient, the idea of change is easier until the first phone call is made, or the first session is scheduled, or the first interpretation is heard. Transference and resistance, the hallmarks of psychoanalysis, are both seminal to the beginning of psychotherapy and symptoms of the fear to leave some familiar way of living.

The beginning of psychotherapy thus establishes a conflict between the therapist and the patient. The patient seeks help to change some undesirable part of his life, some behavior or feeling, some experience of being out of control, or a feeling that something is missing from life. All patients ask for change in one way or another, and each has a special fantasy of how that might occur. Some are sure that simple advice from the very knowledgeable therapist will give new direction, some believe that the therapist's complete understanding will make the cure, some ask for the magic of insight, some believe that they need to change to become worthy of love or respect. It is abhorrent to the new patient to think of repeating anything of the undesirable aspects of his life. Most wish to get on with it, and so often it seems that the therapist stands in the way with all his efforts to find out more information, more details, more history. But these are what therapists use to effect change, very often a change that is different from what the patient first imagined.

So the new patient wants changes and will assert all manner of motivation to make those changes. I have heard statements like "Just tell me what I'm doing wrong," or "Just tell me how to talk to my mother differently," or "Tell me why people never seem to notice my needs," all as if simple words spoken once would make ingrained patterns disappear. Freud (1913) told his patients that it would take him some time to get to know them, and at first this is reasonable enough. But sooner or later the impatience rises again. A compliant patient, for example, illustrates this well in her attempts to do just what she thinks the therapist is asking. The therapist does not advise, so the careful patient sets out to decipher what to do from the nondirective comments of the frustrating therapist. Later she reports her efforts at decoding as well as her attempts at action based on the therapist's hidden advice. All this activity is aimed at change and sadly no change seems to occur. This patient tries hard to make the therapist into a demanding father and to follow his demands in order to feel whole and safe, a method that has proven ineffective in her adult life. It is a pattern resembling that of the smoker trying to quit: one more day of resolve quickly fades as the first and then second cigarettes are lit, and then what difference does one more pack make— "I will renew my resolve tomorrow." The patient's message becomes "What use is therapy if everything I do is just the same as before? I feel as miserable as always and even feel worse since I seem to be failing despite all the good efforts of the therapist." Some ask why the therapist would let this pain happen again. The paradox for the patient is that the old must recur in therapy in order for something new to appear. The past must be enacted in order for the experience of the relationship with the therapist to have effect. Initially, the beginning of something new is immediately threatened just by the potential of starting again—repeating some familiar old experience.

A challenge for the therapist beginning therapy, often as immediately as the first session, is to instill hope in a hopeless person about making changes when, first of all, the deadening effects of repeating one's past must occur. A golf instructor may say, "Take a couple of swings so I can see what you're doing wrong." I don't want to do that since I already feel embarrassed by the sloppiness of my swing or by the fact that just last week she corrected my swing and my arms and body somehow have forgotten what seemed so easy in the last session. For the therapist the undesirable patterns of the patient must be experienced. The only way we can really know what is going on is to become the object of these behaviors and feelings that the patient complains about, and this takes a fair amount of time together, and, for some, even becoming enemies for awhile.

As therapist, I must create a first-session experience with an unknown person that does several crucial things to make therapy seem a worthwhile pursuit. I have to hear what some of the problems are, and get a large-scale map of this person. I have to find the person's pain and hopelessness and help the patient retain that pain as motivation for the therapy. I have to show an ability to understand that pain and convey that understanding in some suitable language. I have to instill a hope of something different and yet make clear that the old ways will remain for some time. I may begin by showing that I will not judge those ways as others have. I have to show that I do not value this person based on his ability to make some change, but that I do value the person, and that I will be able to make use of honesty in our endeavor.

Beginning must be distinguished from starting over. Beginning implies a possibility of something different from before, while starting over is just a repetition. Beginning psychotherapy must contain the hope of creating something different, even if only the therapist holds the hope. For many patients, the unconscious expectation is that therapy is just starting over, another relationship that will take the same path as past relationships. A woman patient caught up in compulsive patterns aptly illustrates starting over. She repeats herself so successfully, so regularly, that it seems there cannot be any growth. She does not recognize those aspects of her experience which, when repeated, fail to reach any hoped-for goal. She simply repeats herself. She tells me of some disappointing experience, quickly finds a point

of self-blame, and asserts that next time she must just try harder.
I imagine that she will try hard but fail to find some way to try
differently. This patient might be surprised to discover that as her
psychotherapist I do not demand she try harder. That surprise
will make for an analytic beginning.

Chapter 2

The Therapist's Stance

I stand at the window of my office feeling a characteristic anxiety about the new patient who is soon to arrive. I go over his name in my mind as a bit of anxiety rises in me to make sure that I address him correctly from the first meeting. I let my mind drift to many associations, thinking back to the phone call with Gregg and wandering to my own issues of the day. I try to recognize any personal anxieties that might impede my attention to this stranger I'm about to meet. I think for a moment that I hope this man can see me, if he decides to continue in therapy, at the open time I have on Tuesdays; I hope he might make my schedule more convenient and be able to pay my regular fee. It is during this time of waiting with its attendant anxieties that I try to track my associations and consider whether or not they refer to anything I already know about this patient or any particular personal conflict that might enter into my first session with him. I begin to analyze my own expectations as I await the in-person portion of our session. I recall, as these very idiosyncratic associations go through my mind, that this man had said on the phone that he had some kind of trouble with relationships. Of course I don't know what this means at this point, but my thoughts go to some other men about Gregg's age I have treated. Single, hard working, very capable in their careers, but unable to make an intimate connection. I think also of their difficulties making a connection with me as their therapist. Some anxiety arises for me as I recall some of the strains these men have presented, in contrast to the more compliant patients who don't threaten to leave over every conflict presented in the therapy. Just before Gregg's time to enter I recognize a familiar excitement about starting with a new patient in psychotherapy. It's an energizing moment, very different from the later times of day-to-day working with a patient I know well. I actually look forward to discovering just what this man will present and just how his relationship to me will unfold, even though I know that if we continue some difficult times will undoubtedly arise between us.

Gregg arrives and switches on the alert light in my waiting room. A little rush of new anxiety runs through me as it probably does Gregg. Even though I'm the therapist I, too, experience anxiety about meeting the stranger on the other side of the door. It's just a minute before the time we have set, so I go to the door hoping to convey to him that I'm ready for our meeting, and that it is important, not squeezed in between many other obligations. As I open the door I see Gregg standing there. I offer my hand for a handshake and say, "I'm Peter Armstrong." He shakes my hand and responds "I'm Gregg Williams." I motion toward my office and say, "The beige chair is mine, please make yourself comfortable anywhere else." He pauses for a moment, and moves toward the couch. He sits looking around my office, apparently orienting himself to this new environment. Gregg says, "This is nice, good view of the river, I bet you like it here." I say briefly, "Thanks, I do." As I sit down I wait just a moment and in my usual manner I say, "We'll meet for forty-five minutes. I'll let you go ahead with what's on your mind. . . ."

THE THERAPIST'S STANCE AS AN ATTITUDE FOR CHANGE

The psychotherapist's stance is the most crucial element of effective psychotherapy. The impact of the therapist and the communication of that stance begin in the first session, even, for that matter, in the first contact, the phone call. In every relationship each person has a stance toward the other. I have a stance toward the store clerk I see each week, toward my family members, and to friends and colleagues. In most of these relationships my stance is an unconscious aspect of my relating, not something I regularly think about or analyze. But because the patient attaches meaning to the therapist's actions and words, and because this is spontaneous and persistent, the analytic therapist must be ready at the first session and all later sessions to consider and analyze his stance.

Every professional has a stance, at the very least a professional, serious, and competent demeanor with which to meet each client. An individual's stance may be distant, warm, inviting, authoritative, friendly, or even unprofessional. Presumably a professional arrives at a stance through trial and error and by observing what makes clients stay, use the services, and express satisfaction. Those who present an unprofessional stance and thereby drive clients away may be demonstrating all sorts of self-defeating dynamics. By comparison, the stance of the analytic therapist is unique in that it is an essential part of the actual service provided. Since the patient immediately begins to attach transference meanings to the therapist, the stance of the therapist must hold a readiness to understand what the patient's meanings are, how those meanings are influenced by the therapist, and how they will be used in the psychotherapy.

Stance as a Part of Treatment

The physician and the attorney have a stance toward their clients, perhaps even a studied stance. The trial attorney may want to convey a stance of being hard driving, ready for the fight, and may constrain any attitude of friendliness that could undermine that stance. It might benefit the attorney to encourage the client's—and others'—awe, in a sense exploiting the authority of his position and his readiness for the client's transference dependence. A male physician may begin to notice that female patients make advances toward him, seemingly without provocation. His authoritative position, the erotic intensity stirred by the physical contact necessary for examination, and the vulnerability of the patient all provide fertile ground for erotic feelings from the patient. For the physician this phenomenon is an impediment to his treatment, not an essential component. The patient's longings may complicate the relationship with an internist or go unnoticed by the surgeon, but they are not the element of the treatment that must be analyzed in order for treatment to progress. The physician and the attorney may exploit or fall prey to the client's transference, but they do not regularly need to experience, understand, and analyze that experience. They may even seek consultation to manage and defuse such transferences, but their work for the client can proceed competently without intrusion into the patient's experience. The analytic therapist's work for the patient cannot, and this is the reason the therapist's stance takes on such importance.

Freud's (1913) paper on beginning treatment took good note of this. He was instructing physicians who were changing from traditional medical practice to the practice of psychoanalysis. Freud recognized that the power of the transference would necessitate a different stance, maybe a unique one, toward patients. Originally, he saw the transference as a great hindrance to the work of psychoanalysis, not unlike the hindrance it might cause the physician or attorney. But the great power of psychoanalysis and psychoanalytic therapies results from Freud's remaking of the transference into the greatest tool of treatment. This was unfamiliar territory for the physicians Freud was addressing, those who early on wanted to learn and employ his new technique: they would have to rethink how they approached the patient in psychotherapy. Today, psychotherapists are trained to perform the work and many of Freud's concepts are an integral part of that training. This readiness for and attitude toward the patient must be carefully considered; the stance with which a therapist approaches the patient, especially in the first meeting, is a crucial part of the treatment.

Psychoanalytic therapies rely on transference. Psychoanalysis proper is most intently focused on the development of transference and the transference neurosis, so that core conflicts, developmental trauma, and failures of empathy are analyzed in the most intensive and experience-near manner possible. In psychoanalytic psychotherapy the transference is regularly met by therapist and patient, and it is often used to further understanding, though perhaps less comprehensively than in formal analysis. Even in therapies that are oriented more toward counseling than analysis, the transference is a key concern for the therapist and the most powerful assessment tool. The analytic therapist's stance is aimed foremost at creating an environment in which the development and use of the transference can occur.

The term *transference* is used in a number of different ways, depending on one's theoretical orientation within psychoanalysis. Throughout this book, in an effort to reach some common ground, the term will refer to the phenomenon through which individuals attach meaning to the actions and words of others. Specifically this is called transference when it occurs in the psychotherapy relationship.

A therapist's stance is a complex integration of theoretical knowledge, extensive training, experience in supervision, and day-to-day work; the many influences of teachers and trainers; and the experience of a wide variety of patients. It is also rooted in personal dynamics and one's self-understanding gained in personal analytic treatment, and is unique, though founded on certain basic principles and guidelines. Psychoanalytic training and training in psychotherapy are broadly aimed at the creation of an analytic stance. Such a stance cannot simply be put in place by education; like the effect of psychoanalytic therapy, one's stance is also the product of experience. As vast and complicated as the idea of stance is, analytic writers and teachers are constantly trying to define its characteristics. For an examination of the first session, some delineation of the therapist's stance is essential.

MODELS, METAPHORS, AND DESCRIPTIONS— THE COMPLEXITIES OF AN ANALYTIC STANCE

Meltzer (1967) states that the analyst must "*preside* over the setting in a way that permits the evolution of the patient's transference" (p. xiii). It is one aspect of the therapist's stance to attend to and arrange this setting, and this especially in the face of a patient's early efforts to undo that setting. From the beginning, we expect to meet the patient's efforts to manage anxiety in ways that will resist the process of the therapy. This is the patient's transference, what Freud (1912a) once considered the greatest obstacle to analysis. But that very enactment will begin to communicate the patient's personality style and manner of engaging the world. The therapist's understanding and adequate management of this dynamic propels the process of therapy and the ultimate understanding of the patient's experience.

The transference must be encouraged, with all of its attendant dependencies, yet without overriding the autonomy of the patient. Consider what a therapist hopes to develop by the end of therapy: an autonomous, independently functioning person. The patient's dependencies are anticipated as an essential part of the experience of therapy. However, the work of the therapy hinges on the reenactment of these dependencies for the purpose of understanding, not to simply replay the dependencies and further incapacitate the patient. Schafer (1983) makes this point in his description of the therapist's work. The therapist analyzes and does not respond in kind. A response in kind is the response that anyone else in the patient's life offers. The therapist does not respond to a person's dependencies with sympathy and assistance, furthering the person's feelings of helplessness and dependency. Rather the analytic stance is one of recognizing the person's autonomy and strengths, allowing for the experience of dependency, and providing a setting in which to analyze that experience. For example, the hostile patient for some underlying reason tends to drive people away from him, or to draw masochistic individuals into his sphere. The analytic therapist does not want to respond in either of these ways, but wants to meet the hostility with a stance that allows for the useful discovery of the underlying reasons.

Greenacre (1954) describes the development of the transference like this:

> If two people are repeatedly alone together, some sort of emotional bond will develop between them. . . . Even if periods of

repeated contact between two individuals do not com-
prise a major part of their time, still such an emotional bond
develops and does so more quickly and more sensitively if the two
persons are *alone* together; . . . Now if both people are adults
but one is troubled and the other is versed in the ways of trouble
and will endeavor to put the torchlight of his understanding at the
disposal of the troubled one, the situation more nearly approxi-
mates that of the analytic relationship. [pp. 671–672]

The patient does not require cajoling to attach transference to
the therapist; this is a spontaneous consequence of sitting in a
room together. But the qualities of a therapist's stance described
by Freud and his successors are aimed at creating the richest
context in which that experience may be observed and allowed to
evolve. In the course of that development some pitfalls exist.
Greenacre (1954) goes on to note the analogy of the psychotherapy relationship to the mother–child relationship and the
tendency of the patient to develop a dependent attitude toward
the therapist. She continues, "How then is the patient's autonomy to be safeguarded and strengthened, in the very situation which might seem to favor its depletion? The chief safeguard
is the analyst's sticking to the work of actually analyzing, and not
serving as guide, model, or teacher, no matter how luring these
roles may be" (p. 673). This is the analytic therapist's stance, one
of guiding the patient toward understanding by the use of
analytic techniques, not by responding as an authority or mentor,
reactions that serve to undermine the patient's autonomy.

Safety

An atmosphere of safety is the overarching quality of the analytic
situation that Schafer (1983) has gathered from all of Freud's
technical papers. Another major aspect of the analytic therapist's
stance has to do with creating that atmosphere. Many factors
detract from or threaten to unsettle the safety of the therapeutic
situation. Schafer refers to the provision of safety from several
potential dangers, including intrusion, loss of confidentiality, and
the patient's fears of being overwhelmed by internal anxieties.
The therapist must be cognizant of these needs for therapy to

proceed. Office arrangements are set to create a sense of safety from intrusion. Therapists go to a great deal of effort to soundproof offices to make sure that private information is not overheard. Yet perhaps the more important dangers are the many intrusions by third parties, family members, and friends, who, in their concern, intrude into the patient's relationship with the therapist. Part of the therapist's stance is to create a strong boundary to keep these intrusions out of the therapy and to explore carefully the need for involvement of others.

Changes in health-care insurance have opened a wide door to intrusion as demands for review of a patient's private information are becoming commonplace. An analytic stance is at least skeptical of the need for such intrusion, and at times strongly resistant to any such intrusion. The atmosphere of safety also includes safety from the sense of being overwhelmed by internal dangers. These dangers are most often related to the very complaints and disorders that the patient brings to therapy. It is the therapist's responsibility to recognize and assess these aspects of the person's personality and to handle such dangers in a competent and professional manner. A constant reconsideration of one's stance toward the patient, and the meanings, idiosyn-cratic as they may be, that the patient attaches to the therapist and the therapist's surroundings, are also part of the therapist's stance. For the first session, the office setting is often enough the first screen onto which the patient projects these fears. The analytic stance is to avoid iatrogenic stimulation of these fears so that a thoughtful exploration can occur.

Confidentiality

Confidentiality does not just protect the patient from the embarrassment of having personal information exposed. In many cases in our society of openness, most revelations by a patient are not so uncommon or strange. We have at times talked of confidentiality as if every patient were revealing perversions or gross dishonesties. Most therapy sessions are filled with rather mundane revelations, even though patients feel shame and embarrassment at the telling. Rather than protecting a patient from shame, which is one of the subjects of the patient's therapy, it is a part of the therapist's stance to protect the patient from the inequity of the relationship necessary for psychotherapy. The patient is the one exposed in psychotherapy. The therapist is holding this information, and by virtue of this unevenness in who is exposed, the therapist gains the balance of power. Confidentiality protects the patient from misuse of that power by the therapist. Consider the nonconfidential relationship we call friendship; here we reveal ourselves evenly because there is no power differential. If my friend abuses my confidences he is no longer my friend—although for that matter I might just as easily abuse his. A good friendship is based on the trust that a friend will not do that and that both parties have some leverage in the relationship by virtue of our equality of purpose. The purpose of privacy in a democracy is to limit the power of a government over its people. The same concern is part of the safety we try to afford patients in psychotherapy. The patient is offered confidence and privacy and the leverage of legal remedy when that privilege is violated.

The privacy of the psychotherapeutic relationship has been eroded by the current health-care system. Privacy has also been eroded significantly by the legal system, which continues to make intrusions into our work—so much so that we are now mandated to explain the limits of confidentiality, an ever-expanding discussion, to each new patient. The details of arranging this with a patient deserve further discussion in the chapters on the contract for psychotherapy. Confidentiality has always been limited—life is not so well defined that all communications of this kind can be fully protected—but the concern here is to provide a first session that is deeply rooted in an atmosphere of safety that the therapist offers as part of the analytic stance.

The analytic therapist's stance is a knowledgeable position from which a variety of sources of danger are understood and dealt with to the extent that the therapist is able. Soundproofing one's office is one aspect of this. When a waiting patient can hear the previous patient speaking, or can hear others outside the office, a sense of safety in confidentiality is not felt. Even if there is no real leak, the feeling of something being unsafe is conveyed.

But danger from the external world comes from other sources as well, in forms perhaps more disturbing and formidable than what can be controlled by sound insulation. Therapists face an increasing need to find ways to maintain the most rigorous confidentiality possible.

Safety and Internal Danger

As psychoanalytic psychotherapy was provided to more primitively organized patients, there also came a growing awareness of the extent and intensity of internal dangers, those anxieties arising in the patient that could be felt to be intolerable, overwhelming, and even life-threatening. These dangers and the threat they present to an atmosphere of safety are of course a major theme of the person's development and therapy. The therapist does not want to convey an uneasiness with such dangers, much less an inability to manage or more importantly to recognize them. The therapist's stance must convey a sense of safety even in the face of extreme fears present and active in the patient's internal world. An ability to convey this competence in the first session is crucial to effecting a relationship for therapy, especially with a person inclined to these fears.

Safety and Play

Another perspective on establishing a safe atmosphere for the patient in therapy rests on the conception of psychotherapy as play. Freud (1914) first spoke of the playground of the transference, but it was Winnicott (1971) who elaborated the concept of psychotherapy as play and as occurring in a play space, an arena between fantasy and reality. The therapist's efforts to create a playground for psychotherapy are discussed in detail by Sanville (1991), who describes the development of a safe place in which the patient can move about. She states its qualities as follows:

> The patient is offered a maximum of freedom to express thoughts, feelings, wishes, and dreads. A special time and place are set aside so as to constitute a sort of interlude from real life, and a sense of secrecy is fostered by the promise of confidentiality.

Order is minimally imposed; ideally, the two participants design the arrangements that they feel will best serve their search. The accepting attitude of the analyst or therapist facilitates a feeling of relative safety to counterbalance the inevitable felt risks. For the therapist the most important rule is respect for the individuality and potential autonomy of the patient, the avoidance of an authoritarian stance and of any exploitation of the transference. . . . Since the therapist has no need to win, the sense of contest is minimized or is more akin to that enjoyed in sports than in battle. Ideally, the patient is enabled to use this relationship to represent other relationships, real and fantasized, and hence learn about them and about the self. [p. 243]

Sanville describes the creation of a playground, a place for the patient's play with fantasies. It must be a safe enough place, and that is the responsibility of the therapist. She emphasizes the therapist's stance of nonauthority, nonintrusiveness, and not having a need to win. In this atmosphere the patient's experience of danger, whether from within or without, can be considered and understood.

THERAPIST QUALITIES

A variety of other qualities are essential to the therapist's stance. Freud provided three guiding concepts for this stance that emphasize the competence of the therapist: "The treatment must be carried through in a state of abstinence" (1915, p. 383), ". . . take as a model in psycho-analytic treatment the surgeon who puts aside all his own feelings, including that of human sympathy, and concentrates his mind on one single purpose, that of performing the operation as skillfully as possible" (1912b, p. 327), and "The physician should be impenetrable to the patient, and, like a mirror, reflect nothing but what is shown to him" (1912b, p. 331). These metaphors for the therapist's activity have often been repeated—to the extent that, at times in the history of psychoanalysis, their utility has been lost to concretization. Stone (1961) reviewed these aspects of the analytic situation in a monograph that attempted to rescue Freud's metaphors and rehumanize their use. He gives extensive consideration to the history and development of the analyst–patient relationship, and describes the development of the analyst's stance as revealed in Freud's technical papers. Stone traces the history of the physician as analyst from Freud's early use of hypnosis and suggestion to his later formulations. Early on, the use of hypnosis held the physician in his traditional position as a benign authority, trusted to do only good for the patient, not involved in the suffering of the patient, but intent on relieving that suffering from a position of knowledge and power. Stone shows that even with Dora (1905), Freud's sense of transference was underdeveloped, and that the use of suggestion and direction from his position as authority was the effective force of the treatment. Emphasis on the development of the transference through the patient's active involvement of free association came only later. The patient's responsibility for free association changes the position of the analyst in the relationship to one of partnership. The analyst does not "work on" the patient as a surgeon works on a person under anesthesia; rather, the patient is working as a responsible party in the analytic relationship and must provide some entrance for the analyst into her inner world through the production of free associations. Over time these metaphors for the analyst's stance became codified as invariable rules for the conduct of psychoanalysis. Stone (1961) seeks to adjust this rigid use of Freud's metaphors by defining more specific guidelines, and showing Freud's intentions and illustrations of the principles. He then describes later abuse of these ideas, particularly as they evolved into rules. An important purpose of Stone's writing was to assert the essential meaning and value of these metaphors, to remove the rule-like rigidity with which they came to be applied, and to find a place for the communication of the analyst's humanity within this intimate, professional relationship.

Abstinence

Abstinence was introduced by Freud (1915) in an unfortunately dogmatic manner. It referred primarily to "physical erotic cravings," but more broadly to many other desires. Abstinence was intended to allow the drives to maintain their force so that analysis could occur. In this respect, the stance that Freud encourages is similar to Schafer's (1983) principle that the analyst *analyzes* rather than providing a variety of other interventions and actions characteristic of a professional relationship. Stone (1961) describes the way abstinence became a rule of analysis, and how that rule then was used to forbid some expected, and even necessary, gratifications of the analytic relationship.

The key feature relevant to the therapist's stance is the focus on where the motive force for treatment lies. In classical analysis it has often been thought to lie in the patient's suffering— sometimes brought on by the therapist's refusal to gratify the patient. Stone (1961) encourages a softening of the rigid application of the abstinence rule, and asserts that no lessening of the strength or availability of the transference results. It is my understanding that the purpose of abstinence is solely to create an analytic situation, one that allows for analysis rather than reenactment by the therapist. As Schafer (1983) suggests, if the analyst responds in kind, that is, simply as another object in the patient's life, no analysis has occurred. Abstinence thus allows the patient a new response, one predicated on an experience that brings the behavior or impulse or conflict into an arena that makes conscious understanding and working through possible.

The Surgeon Model

The surgeon model (Freud 1912b) instructs the analyst to put aside personal feelings and sympathies in order to concentrate on the skillful performance of the operation. This vivid picture of the forbearance of the analyst evolved into an attitude of coldness. Stone (1961) reconsiders this recommendation and provides a more balanced understanding of the surgeon model. It is not that the analyst stops feeling, but that personal feelings are subordinated to the skillful rendering of the work. With the refinement of the concept of countertransference and the development of its use, especially with more primitively organized

patients, the analyst's feelings in fact become an important aspect
of his technical skill. But the use of countertransference does not
in any way suggest a "response in kind" as Schafer (1983, p. 8)
puts it. Rather, the countertransference experience is an internal
"response in kind" that the analyst uses to further understanding, not as a method of directing action toward the other person.

The Mirror Reference

The mirror reference (Freud 1912b) is a recommendation to the
analyst to focus on the patient's conflicts and avoid disclosure of
his own. This has always been a principle of analytic therapies and
part of a professional stance. In his response to this metaphor, the
analyst mirrors the patient's conflicts and remains personally
opaque to the patient. This idea became rigid in its overinter-
pretation. Stone (1961) mentions those analysts who attempted
to hide all expressions of their own personality, even to the extent
of decorating their offices in the most bland ways. But as
Greenson (1967) comments, this only projects another sort of
self expression to the patient. Probably Stone would agree that
the mirror metaphor was not intended by Freud to hide the
analyst's personal expressions of one sort or another, but rather
to emphasize the analyst's attention to the patient's conflicts, and
to keep the analyst's conflicts sufficiently in check so as to not
interrupt the growth of the patient's transference. The many
benign expressions of the analyst's personality, in Stone's opinion, did not obstruct the growth and use of the transference. In
considering the therapist's stance I will discuss my view that the
therapist's personal style and the inevitable expression of the
therapist's personality are not merely benign, but an integral part
of the therapist's stance, and that they must be understood and
analyzed by the therapist along with all the other parts of the
relationship that come under scrutiny of the therapist's self
analysis of countertransference.

Stone (1961) reviews these concepts and the manner in which
they have been incorporated into analytic work. He notes how
easily these principles became rigid modes of treatment that
eroded the sense of human presence in the analytic stance. To

temper these rules, using Freud's own recommendations, Stone cites Freud's emphasis on building rapport and giving hope of relief of suffering, much as Schafer (1983) asserts that the therapist "aims to be helpful" (p. 11).

Schafer (1983) describes several other qualities of the therapist's stance, including neutrality, the avoidance of either/or thinking, and the recognition that the analyst analyzes, rather than performing other activities. Among these, neutrality has recently come under fire as an unquestioned analytic attitude, and rightly so, since it is a quality so ripe for abuse. Psychotherapy is a human and humane treatment that is damaged in its effect if it is provided in a rigid, mechanistic manner. Many writers have reminded therapists that psychotherapy can be provided in a highly expert and professional manner without lessening the compassion and humanity a patient needs to feel from the therapist.

Neutrality

Schafer's (1983) standard of neutrality applies to several aspects of the analytic therapy. First, the therapist is neutral toward the various aspects of the patient's personality—the id, ego, and superego. The effort here is to allow all conflictual material to emerge over time without bias. The recognition of time is pertinent here, since the understanding is that in the analytic setting material is presented that will require time to be fully developed, and that over time what is emphasized in a patient's material will change. Secondly, the therapist remains neutral and nonjudgmental toward the individuals in the patient's life, recognizing that the patient's presentation of these persons may contain identifications and projections, and further, that the patient in the consulting room is the one under scrutiny, not the others in his life. Finally, the therapist subordinates his personality, including wishes, values, expectations, and so on.

Contemporary analysts have questioned some of these traditionally held qualities of the therapist. The evolution of thought about the analyst's position toward the patient has arisen from efforts to increase the safety of the analytic situation, and has often come from therapists' efforts to make analytic therapy available to a wider range of patients. These developments also represent changes in philosophies underlying the work today. The controversies involve the intricacies of psychoanalytic theory and influences on technique, questions that are beyond the scope of this book. Mitchell (1998) has described the philosophical differences between contemporary relational ideas and classical analytic thought. He challenges the authority of the analytic therapist to know what is in the patient's mind and proposes new ways of considering the therapist's expertise and value for the patient. This perspective places the therapist in an expert role, but one of collaboration and guidance to self-reflection. These ideas challenge the traditionally held conceptions of neutrality and objectivity, and in fact the therapist is no longer regarded as objective at all. The therapist's experience is more important to the process of therapy than ever before.

Stolorow and Atwood's (1997) paper deals with the myth of the neutral analyst. Writing from an intersubjective systems approach, they conclude that "interpretations are always sugges-tions, transference is always contaminated, analysts are never objective" (p. 431). They offer another stance, which is de-scribed as "empathic-introspective inquiry" (p. 431). Again, the theoretical underpinnings of these ideas are not in the scope of a discussion of the first session. The approach, however, supports all of the general characteristics of stance that I have discussed earlier. In fact these contemporary approaches make an even greater effort to create for the patient an environment in which understanding can occur; they are nonjudgmental, nonauthori-tarian and encourage a wide-ranging inquiry into one's thoughts and fantasies.

Length of Time

A key point of analytic therapy is that a significant period of time will be necessary for any clear understanding to be made of the patient's conflicts. Perhaps an attitude of neutrality, as Schafer (1983) states it, is most pertinent for the first session, since so little is known. Many patients come to the first session in hopes that the therapist will quickly be able to decipher what is going on and give advice, authoritarian diagnosis, and other rapid responses to their problems. A sense of neutrality slows us down and must be conveyed to the patient through our stance in these early contacts. I find a particular demand of new patients is that the therapist take the patient's side against some person who is felt to be treating the new patient unfairly. The analytic stance of neutrality directs our attention back to the patient, not to the analysis of others, and onto the patient's inner world, away from the concerns and values of the therapist. While the current emphasis on countertransference and intersubjective experience has brought the concept of neutrality up for question, at least as it has been historically understood, these are advances of our technique, and have added to the humanness of analytic treatments. These ideas press us to reject neutrality as requiring a distance from the patient's experience, or as antithetical to the relationship that is formed in the analytic experience.

Tolerating Ambiguity

The theory of psychoanalysis is incompatible with viewing problems, conflicts, or objects in the person's life in black-and-white terms. The work of therapy involves tolerance of ambiguity, and part of the therapist's task is aiding this tolerance. Schafer (1983) states,

> If one takes seriously these principles of overdetermination, multiple function and ambivalence, one can only judge it to be a failure of the analytic attitude to encounter an analyst speaking of what something "really" means. For to speak of the "real" meaning disregards these principles. The fact that one has discerned *further* meaning, *weightier* meaning, *more disturbing* meaning, *more archaic* meaning, or *more carefully disguised* meaning than that which first met the eye or the ear does not justify the claim that one has discovered the ultimate truth that lies behind the world of appearances—the "real" world. . . . The analytic attitude will be evident in the analyst's making a more modest as well as sounder claim, namely, that a point has now been reached in the analytic dialogue where reality must be

formulated in a more subtle and complex manner than it has been
before. [p. 8]

New patients often think in a black-and-white manner, demonstrating rigidities that defend against the fears they have
confronted in their lives and problems. It is the work of therapy
to explore these fears and problems and to help the patient to
develop the tolerance that Schafer describes. Patients also seek
direction and advice, often in the first session, as if some simple
answers will solve their problems. The analytic stance of avoiding
either/or thinking begins the process toward greater tolerance of
the ambiguities inherent in living and growth in one's ability to
make good judgments in life.

Schafer (1983) also remarks that "The analyst's focus is on the
interpretation of psychical reality. With this focus the analyst is
not obliged to respond in kind to the analysand's emotional
overtures" (p. 8). I believe this to be a key element of the
therapist's stance and a defining feature of what constitutes
analytic therapy versus many other types of therapy, and what
distinguishes the transference experience for the patient from
that of simply another relationship full of the troubles he is trying
to resolve. This focus makes it a relationship in which understanding and change can occur. Therapy requires a certain
frustration and constraint, as has been noted, but the frustration
of the therapist's spontaneous reaction to the patient's presentation is the basis for the growth of the transference and for the
ultimate interpretation of that experience. When a therapist
responds in kind she becomes merely another object in that
patient's life, and little understanding ensues. Freud (1910)
addressed this issue in his paper "Observations on 'Wild' Psycho-
Analysis," in which he criticized a physician's use of analytic
theory to advise a patient on what changes she should make in
her life. Freud shows the resistances that emerged in the patient
but, most pertinently, criticized the complete lack of analysis
evident in such advice. Analysis is about the uncovering and
understanding of underlying motivations. It cannot be used to
quickly assess and direct a person to new forms of behavior. The
behavioral changes will arise from the careful analysis and

understanding of the psychical reality. While a patient's urgent call for help will stir the therapist to some other function than the one at hand, response in kind is another sort of enactment by the therapist, one that is not an act of analysis. The therapist's stance must demonstrate this from the outset of therapy.

The Therapist's Attitude

"For the analyst, analyzing is not an alternative to being helpful, it is the analytic way of being helpful. It is just that the manifest gains produced by this effort to be helpful may not be immediate, unambiguous, of an expected or easily recognizable sort, or instantly responded to by the analysand with unbounded joy" (1983, p. 13). This statement of Schafer's emphasizes the importance of a positive attitude toward the patient's presentation, even when the presentation is one of resistance and reluctance to change inefficient and neurotic ways of dealing with living. The analytic therapist is aware that the slowness to change itself is a product of the very conflicts and compromises that come under analysis, and that if the therapy is appropriate, then analysis of those conflicts is the most helpful means of achieving growth. Analytic therapy is a treatment first—never simply a research tool for the therapist—and helpfulness is a goal. But in conjunction with the above attributes of the therapist's stance, helpfulness occurs within the context of analytic theory and technique. The patient's wish for some other activity on the part of the analytic therapist must always be seen within the scope of the effort to understand the underlying nature of what motivates that desire, not a simple response in kind to the patient's wishes. This is analytic helpfulness.

Authority and Expertise

The discussion of the therapist's stance seems to present a polarity that many writers have struggled to define and translate into analytic technique. The therapist must conduct the psychotherapy with expertise and at the same time encourage and support the patient's autonomy and, in effect, the patient's expertise for her own life. All of the above emphasizes that the therapist is competent and an expert in the provision of therapy and the management of the therapeutic process. This can erode into the mechanistic, authoritative stance that Stone (1961) attempted to correct. The therapist must be an authority about the workings of psychotherapy without becoming an authority over the patient. The therapist's task is to expertly create an analytic situation without overriding the patient's autonomy, at the same moment that the patient's transference may well pressure the therapist to unknowingly become that authority.

The therapist's stance is one of expertise. Competence gained through hard efforts at training, education, and self-analysis is demanded of the therapist. It is through this expertise that the therapist manages a treatment that provides a person with an avenue to autonomy, independence, and greater self-reliance. It is the complexity of this task that places so much weight on the nature of the therapist's stance in the first session and in each subsequent session until termination of the treatment.

To be an effective psychotherapist one must persistently evolve an analytic stance. That position and attitude is created in small steps with each patient and with each session. The work of analytic therapy places a great responsibility on the therapist to continue a process of self-analysis and growth. At the first session, all of the many characteristics and aspects of the therapist's stance immediately come into play. One cannot meet a patient with a stance that is antithetical to the work and hope to return to an adequate position with the patient at some later point. Remember Meltzer's (1967) admonition to preside over the work; it will do no good to start in a position requiring campaigning later on. I believe he means for the therapist to start out presiding in this way. But what does this mean to the first session? The first session, as Ogden (1989) has asserted, is no more or less analytic therapy than any later session. However, the first session is unique in that it is a meeting of two strangers. Strangers are apt to miscommunicate or misunderstand much more readily than two individuals who are familiar with each other's ways. Because the potential for the therapist to be misunderstood and even short circuit the beginning of the therapy is clearly greater in the first session, the therapist must pay particular attention to his stance at this moment of meeting.

Consider an interaction long into a treatment. I make an offhand joking remark to a patient, perhaps to acknowledge a long-familiar resistance, perhaps to lighten some aspect of the patient's depression, perhaps because I was in a lighthearted mood from the previous patient. All no doubt with some as yet hidden countertransference meaning. Instead of hearing my conscious meaning of a joking remark, the patient today hears an insult. She is offended and does not speak for several minutes. My light-hearted mood is quickly erased and I am rapidly reviewing my associations for the source of my comment and the patient's hurt. The patient does not leave the room, though she might fantasize finding a new therapist or screaming at me in anger or hiding in silence. Over the course of the session we begin to think together about her hurt, my remark, and so on. We take an offhand remark, a countertransference enactment, into the analysis and we are able to negotiate this session because we have a long history together, an alliance that saves the day. But the first session does not allow for such forgiveness of mistakes; it is a time for particular attention to miscommunication.

About fifteen minutes into the session, Gregg is involved in telling me about his life, and has begun to touch on some concerns that stir affect in his voice and facial expression. He speaks of an ex-girlfriend who broke up with him about a year ago and for just a moment it seems that tears might come to his eyes. He manages to hold back the expression of his feelings by subtly shifting the subject away from his hurt about this woman leaving him. As he continues on he interrupts himself and asks, "Are you recording this session? I just saw a light on your desk that looks like my dictating machine in the office. I think you should tell me you're recording the session and not just go ahead without asking." I'm a bit startled at the abruptness with which he brings this up and even with his thought that I'm recording the session. I never record in session, I don't even take notes in the session. I'm listening intently to Gregg and it strikes me that he has become agitated by this and has shown an expression of anger that is in contrast to how he has been talking with me. I realize quickly that he's referring to my telephone, which has a signal light in place of a ringer tone. Somehow the way I set the phone down and the way he's settled back into my couch has put the light in his range of vision, one not typically in other patients' line of sight. I pause before responding, even though Gregg's tone of voice has a certain urgency in it. He could even be thinking that I have violated his sense of privacy and disclosure to a degree that he might abort the therapy with me. Much later in a therapy I would be inclined to pursue a patient's associations to the idea of being recorded without permission. At that time the patient and I would already be familiar with the idea of associating to experiences and fantasies rather than insisting with urgency on changing something. I think that Gregg must know that I'm not recording his session and I must convey this in a way that he can take in even with the agitation he feels. Then I also might be able to demonstrate something of the way therapy goes by directing him to some of his associations and feelings about this event and about me. I say to Gregg . . .

MISSTEPS AND MISCOMMUNICATIONS

From the first moment of meeting a patient I want to demonstrate that this session will be like all others to come. The unique aspect of the first session is that the two individuals are strangers, with no history, no feeling about each other beyond the fantasies that have begun around the phone call and other indirect information either has received. This is fertile ground for misunderstanding.

Analytic therapists must consider what will convey an unwanted message. Consider what a new patient might imagine if he were to walk into a therapist's waiting area, full of first-session anxiety, not knowing what to expect, but having succeeded in arriving on time. The therapist's door is open. The therapist is talking on the phone, notices the patient's arrival, and motions the person to enter. Consider the first message this therapist gives. Have you ever tried to have lunch with someone who is chatting on a cell phone? What have your own feelings been when waiting for a professional appointment where the doctor or lawyer or accountant has let you sit for twenty minutes past the meeting time, as if something else is more important? What, too, could this psychotherapist's action imply about how private these sessions will be?

Simple actions, some even tolerated in the day-to-day functioning of working society, begin to form a fantasy of psychotherapy for the patient that will be difficult to undo. If we hope to convey that the patient's concerns are the focus of treatment, we must greet the patient in a manner that will not obstruct that message. If we intend to make time an important part of the therapy, for example that missed sessions and lateness have meanings and consequences, we must treat time as an important matter from the outset. The feelings I have about the attorney I consult who comes twenty minutes late to an appointment may not enter into the work she will perform for me in the same way they will into the transference relationship the therapist builds with a patient. However, I may not return to that attorney.

The challenge in the first session is for the therapist to foresee what actions and words might become misunderstood by this stranger, before any depth of relationship has created a foundation for exploration.

Later in the relationship, the demands of life and the pressures of countertransference may create all manner of circumstances. Every therapist has come late to a session, forgotten a session, or booked two patients at the same time. But in the midst of a relationship with a history of sensitivity and positive experience, the therapist's missteps may be adequately explored and the results will be less threatening to the continuation of the psychotherapy than in the first moments of meeting.

Perhaps the actual place where the therapy will occur is the immediate screen onto which the new patient projects first-session meanings. We rightly take care to soundproof our offices, but we must also consider what a new patient sees as he first arrives. Often we do not conduct our work in the fashion of

other professionals. Many psychotherapists do not have a receptionist or do not have an open door to clients. Do we create
confusion for the patient first entering? The veteran patient
knows to enter the waiting room and switch on the alert button
or whatever, but does the new patient, unless given a bit of
instruction over the phone?

A colleague of mine sought treatment at one time from a
recommended therapist of extensive experience. At the time my
colleague was in a period of some distress, yet she was a therapist
herself and had significant prior experience in psychotherapy. At
the end of the session she stood to leave the office and noticed
that there were two doors, one by which she had entered.
Thinking that the other door was an exit that would not go
through the waiting room she queried if that was the one to use.
The therapist made no reply, apparently holding to the rule of
abstinence. She took the other door only to find it a dead-end
hallway with a locked door at the end, and had to return in
awkwardness through the therapist's office. This created an
experience that did not feel safe. She wondered how she could
work with this therapist in a state of mind in which she needed
some feeling of security and a sense that this therapist would be
able to guide her through the troubles she was experiencing. She
found another therapist and did not return. Another patient
might have become discouraged about the whole project.

Our office, the setting in which therapy will occur, is one
consideration in the creation of an atmosphere of safety for the
patient. Because the setting in which psychotherapy is conducted
differs from many professional offices with which a naive patient
may be familiar, we need to pay attention to how the potential
patient will experience this aspect of the therapy office. Early in
training we are told to observe the new patient's choice of seat in
an office. Does she sit distant from the therapist or near? Do
couples sit together or apart? But it is not so clear where the
therapist sits. A man came into my office for a first session and sat
in my chair. It was not that the chair was bigger or more
comfortable, he just chose that chair; it was not clear that it was
mine. Unlike the attorney's office where the professional's chair
is behind the desk, my office is more like a living room and this

patient made himself comfortable. We experienced the awkward moment of my having to ask him to move. I now tell new patients that the beige chair is mine and they are welcome to sit wherever else looks comfortable. I make an early effort to avoid this moment of awkwardness. Future interactions will present enough difficulties, but they will occur in the balance of a working relationship.

These are concrete examples of early miscommunications, trivial perhaps but offering analogies to the many chances to create a misunderstanding—often out of our routines, which blind us to how new this experience is for the patient and how much anxiety the patient may attach to various actions. The setting of psychotherapy is intended to be somewhat undefined. We try to create a setting onto which the patient projects inner experience, and we hope to observe from the outset the resources or lack of resources the patient has to manage anxiety. But even minimal attention to how the setting might overly confuse or frustrate the patient will go a long way toward creating the sense of safety necessary for the person to use the relatively undefined space.

There are endless possibilities for therapist and new patient misunderstandings. In any given first session the vagaries of the therapist's life may make for an unfortunate miscommunication. It is when these occur regularly that the therapist must wonder about the nature of his approach to the patient. The new therapist who loses most of his patients after a session or two does well to consult about these patterns, or to enter psychotherapy to understand more about what happens.

As much attention as we give to how we begin or as careful as we might be in setting the therapy in motion, there are aspects of the therapy setting that will necessarily miscommunicate or be taken in by the patient's transference from the outset. As I have suggested, the way we arrange our offices, answer our phones, and receive our patients is markedly different from such routines in the medical profession at large, and are thus often confusing to the patient. I recently met a new patient, one naive to psychotherapy. Her first words, with surprise in her voice were, "What about the paperwork?,"—because it was something she was used to being greeted with in her doctor's office. However, that's not the way I greet a patient for psychotherapy.

Policy Intrusions

Just as disturbing as any of the above issues are the increasing policies to which psychotherapy has become subject, and the procedures we are mandated to conform with, which might be misunderstood by the patient. I refer here to the demands for explanations of disclosure, and even demands that we announce our fee over the phone. Two specific aspects of policy intrusions deserve attention, each with its own arena for miscommunication. First, laws are increasingly directing our work in ways that create misunderstanding for the new patient. And second, the current use of many types of insurance reimbursement further causes us to limit some of the important parameters of the psychotherapy relationship.

Changes in the laws and ethical codes regulating psychotherapy have affected the first session in several dramatic ways. Increasingly there is a demand for written consent to treatment and documentation of the contract for psychotherapy. In the contract, the therapist is expected to explain all manner of circumstances and events that might occur as a result of the psychotherapy. Theoretically this cannot be done; one cannot predict the possibilities of human relationships, and those who have attempted to predict criminal and violent behavior have long known this. But, along with other professions, we have become vulnerable to the demands of a consumer-oriented society, one that makes demands of a kind that are often the very reason why psychotherapy is needed.

It is the responsibility of each therapist in each profession to know what expectations are made by his licensing boards, ethical codes, and the laws governing the profession. But to carry out those demands without consideration of their effect conflicts with the analytic therapist's stance. The courts and licensing boards are ostensibly motivated to require more and more documentation and to obtain informed consent to protect the unwary consumer. But the need for these protections arose from only a small percentage of cases, injured patients, or unethical therapists. It is the therapist's responsibility to consider what the experience is for the patient sitting in the office at any particular moment—and what is best for that patient.

What does it signal to a new patient when a therapist begins to explain when confidentiality will be breached? Does it stir fears and iatrogenic resistance in the patient who, for example, has been a victim of child abuse, that this will once again become public? Surely such statements by a therapist will interfere with the openness of a person who has been violent or suicidal. The therapist working with specific populations, extremely disturbed patients, or perpetrators of child abuse will have to introduce these matters into the initial session of treatment. While often these treatments are not conducted as traditional therapies, the therapist must still be aware of the influence of calling for such informed consent. More important, what do these statements stir in the fantasy of the patient who is not so disturbed, not a victim or perpetrator of abuse, but who is seeking therapy for other concerns?

An issue adjunct to the informed consents we are mandated to obtain is that of the growing quantity of paperwork that is provided to the new patient. It is becoming common for psychotherapists to require signed consent forms, apparently to ensure that the patient is certifying that she has read and understands all of the statements they contain. While the law and our licensing boards may require this, consider what message we send the new patient. Do we imply that all of the processes of psychotherapy can be foretold? Can we explain in any understandable way the emotional pain that might be experienced during the course of psychotherapy?

The pain experienced in psychotherapy is not like that experienced in surgery or an illness. In many cases, physical pain is a side effect of the treatment; it often slows recovery, and for the most part medicine is aimed at alleviating that pain. Not so with psychotherapy. The pain of psychotherapy is an essential experience of the process. Many patients take a long time to open themselves to the emotional pain associated with childhood events. The very process of experiencing that pain and understanding the effects of defending against the experience is the work of psychotherapy and its movement toward greater freedom and a wider range of emotional experience. Can the psychotherapist really provide informed consent that is modeled on medical consents? And if so, do we send an unwanted message to the new, possibly naive patient?

Contemporary psychotherapists must grapple with these very difficult demands of current law, ethics, clinical technique, and the ubiquity of transference. Some things that can be done in a first session involve a careful look at what messages are sent by the actions we take around these legal mandates. Part of my stance as a therapist is that the patient's concerns will be foremost in our sessions and that the relationship is experienced *in* the psychotherapy sessions. Freud (1913) warned us of patients who will try to keep some aspect of their lives outside of the therapy session. Therapists may do the same. The effect of these consents and related paperwork must be considered by the therapist. Patients no doubt will say that they are used to all the paperwork because they see it with other professionals. But the psychotherapy relationship is unique, and the unconscious effects of these demands will arise.

In my work I have tried to keep the paperwork out of the relationship, in hopes of conveying the most human of professional contacts and to demonstrate that everything that will go on in the therapy will go on by talk between me and the patient. Others have found various forms utilitarian in their work and have found ways to use the forms without conveying impersonality. Therapists must, however, consider their own defensive use of forms. The worst situation involves the therapist who uses a form to describe money and scheduling policies that she feels anxiety about discussing directly. This inevitably sends the message that these matters are somehow not part of the therapy, or makes it evident that the therapist is deflecting some anxiety-stimulating issues—allowing the patient to do so as well at some point. These matters are an essential part of the therapy and must not be left outside the consulting room. Equally offensive, however, is the therapist who presents the paperwork and sheet of rules for the patient before they even meet person to person.

This in my mind undermines the very basis of the therapy relationship, a face-to-face human experience that is guided by the coming together of two individuals and the many assessments that arise from the struggle to fit. It is also bad business. Do you really want to be judged by your paperwork? It is far more preferable, in any situation that requires an ongoing contact, to meet in such a way that early assessments can be made first; then the policies can be discussed and negotiated.

I have gotten to my office enough ahead of time to be sure nothing will cause me to be late to this first session. I automatically check to make sure that my office is in order, but I take a bit more care than with an ongoing patient. I look in the waiting room to make sure the latest solicitors have not left unrequested brochures. I look over the physical setting where we will be working to assure myself that it will appear as I wish, and that my office will present itself as a safe enough place for this work.

As I wait for Gregg to arrive, I allow my thoughts and associations to flow into my awareness. One aspect of my analytic stance is that even at this early moment I begin to consider what these associations mean to me personally, as a part of my ongoing self-analysis, and in considering the patient. I am interested in what might be useful about this patient even given our brief phone contact. I follow, as best I can, what fantasies he has already stirred in me. Additionally, I follow up on what aspects of my own internal process might intrude on Gregg's therapy, even his first session. I think about whether I can bring my full attention to the task of this session, and whether I can readily agree to continue with Gregg if he decides that's what he wants during our first session. In short, I begin to exercise my analytic stance even as I wait for the patient. As therapist, I hold this attitude with the expectation that I will take this same stance into the session, the first one and all the others, to attempt the same quality of analysis with this new patient. As I invite Gregg into the room, I am hopeful, and intend to give him a great deal of freedom in which to express himself and to begin to explore the workings of his mind. I hope to give him at least the same freedom I feel in the exploration of my own mind. This is a part of how I hope to convey to Gregg and any other new patient the process of therapy, a process of discovery in a safe and free environment.

TRANSLATING STANCE INTO FIRST SESSION TECHNIQUE

A few analytic writers have revealed their first sessions, and I present all of the examples I found. In each of the following cases the writer demonstrates his or her stance, as illustrated by a first-session excerpt. These examples show specific ways in which the writer translates a unique stance into first-session actions. Each therapist pays attention to the underlying analytic issues of transference, countertransference, and resistance, but handles those themes in uniquely personal ways.

Working Together: Hilde Bruch

Bruch's (1974) book *Learning Psychotherapy* is written primarily as an introduction to psychotherapy for beginning therapists. The title of her chapter on the first session, "When Strangers Meet," suggests an equality between therapist and patient in their being unknown to one another and facing anxieties inherent in first meetings. She emphasizes an attitude of empathy in seeking to understand the patient. Bruch gives a first session example from a case in which she was a consultant. It is the treatment of a young schizophrenic girl that is the basis of the book *I Never Promised You a Rose Garden*. This was the beginning of an especially difficult case of a woman who had experienced numerous prior treatments. The beginnings are further complicated since the patient at first mistakes the doctor for a housekeeper. Bruch quotes:

> They went into a sunny room and the Housekeeper-Famous-Doctor turned, saying, "Sit down. Make yourself comfortable." There came a great exhaustion and when the doctor said, "Is there anything you want to tell me?" a great gust of anger, so that

Deborah stood up quickly . . . "All right—you'll ask me questions and I'll answer them—you'll clear up my 'symptoms' and then send me home . . . *and what will I have then?*"

The doctor said quietly, "If you did not really want to give them up, you wouldn't tell me . . . Come, sit down. You will not have to give up anything until you are ready, and then there will be something to take its place . . . Do you know why you are here?" [p. 16]

There follows an outburst of a list of self-belittling descriptions, with expressed anger that her complaints had been rated imaginary. The patient feels that she has spoken her true feelings for the first time.

The doctor said simply, "Well, that seems to be quite a list. Some of these things, I think, are not so, but we have a job cut out for us." [p. 16]

The report describes a further volley of the patient's expression of fears and the doctor's empathic and hopeful responses. She does not minimize the patient's difficulties, she does not collude with the patient's hopelessness, and she does not engage with the patient's efforts to see her as every other therapist who has failed to help the young girl.

The rope tightened. Fear was flowing wildly in Deborah's head, turning her vision gray. "You're saying what they all say—phony complaints about nonexistent sicknesses."

"It seems to me that I said you are very sick, indeed."

"Like the rest of them here?" . . .

"Do you mean to ask me if I think you belong here, if yours is what is called a mental illness? Then the answer is yes. I think you are sick in this way, but with your very hard work here and with a doctor's working hard with you, I think you can get better." [p. 17]

The famous Doctor was Frieda Fromm-Reichmann. Bruch goes on to report that years later Fromm-Reichmann would review the beginnings of the treatment with the patient. With

certainty about the reason treatment was able to begin with
success, the girl reminded the doctor that she had used the word
"us" when talking about how treatment would work. This is
what captured this girl's interest in the treatment. She says:
"Here was somebody who did not think she could cure me, or
do it for me, but who said, 'We'll do it together'" (p. 17).

The emphasis here is on the "we" of the therapy. Bruch
(1974) values this highly as the foundation upon which treatment will progress and succeed. Bruch sees the ability of the
therapist to empathically communicate understanding to the
patient as a key to the success of the treatment. Her intention is
not to begin therapy with all the technique and theory that will
be required in the coming stages, but to begin with a foundation
of empathy that creates the safe space in which the patient can
work. Throughout her description of the initial interview and
recommendations for the therapist's activity, the underlying
stance is one of mutual effort at understanding. This therapist
does not take a position of authority over the patient's experience
or desires, but invites a collaboration. Bruch encourages careful
assessment of the patient's needs and wishes for therapy and the
patient's ability to engage in it. For example, later in the chapter,
she notes the importance of a careful exploration of the patient's
ability to pay for treatment, and one instance of a failure to
thoroughly understand the patient's situation in setting a fee too
high. Her chapter is written to beginning therapists and thus
comments on a number of elementary issues; however the
emphasis is one of humanness and an effort on the part of the
therapist to present in a genuine and not artificially professional
manner that provides the patient with an environment in which
the understanding of the many difficult conflicts and problems
can occur. One gets the sense that all of the complex difficulties
of analytic technique, and the analysis of the patient's many
deeply felt problems, move more comfortably and successfully
with such a stance.

A Place to Search For Meaning—Thomas Ogden

Ogden's (1989) overriding theme is the search for the meaning
of the patient's experience. The intensity with which he engages

in this search is captured in his statement, "Everything that the analyst does in the first face-to-face analytic session is intended as an invitation to the patient to consider the meaning of his experience" (p. 170). He goes on to explain his efforts to direct the patient's attention toward things that have long been considered obvious and unworthy of new observation, and to create an atmosphere of safety and openness for the inquiry into meanings. In addition to his view of the analytic experience as one of searching for meanings, he encourages the analyst, especially the experienced analyst, to remain open to the discovery or rediscovery of these experiences as new. He de-emphasizes expectation and prediction in favor of a readiness to surprise. Underpinning the search for meaning is the therapist's ability to experience with the patient each potential avenue to new understanding. The following case example demonstrates his approach to the first session.

The patient is a man in his mid-forties, engaged in a successful career. He comes to Ogden because he is experiencing fears of dying and is preoccupied with these fantasies and his concerns for what will happen to his young, hearing-impaired daughter if he were to die. He is aware that his fears are exaggerated, but this does not quell them. The fears have plagued him since he was a child and he relates them in part to the harsh ways his father treated him. Ogden's report goes on:

> Mr. H. told me that his success at work seemed unreal to him. He felt as if he had to be continually preparing for the day when he would no longer be able to function. As a result, he hoarded every penny that he earned. He gave several examples of feeling dangerously depleted when he spent money. I then said that it seemed as if he was suggesting that the idea of paying for analysis would be frightening because it would mean giving up one of the few sources of protection that he felt he had. Mr. H. smiled and said that he had thought a great deal about this, and that the prospect of paying for analysis felt to him like a blood-letting in which there would be a race between his "cure" and his bleeding to death. [p. 178]

Ogden takes this early opportunity to demonstrate how the patient's present experience may be worked with in the coming analysis. It is a stance that pays great heed to the focus of analysis on the immediate experience as well as on the potential meaning in anything the patient presents. He continues with the second session in which

> [H]e was perspiring and seemed to have been waiting for me like a man anxiously awaiting some terribly important piece of news, perhaps a verdict. Immediately upon entering my room, he walked across the room and reached for the phone, saying, "I locked my keys in the car and so if it's all right, I'd like to call my wife to ask her to meet me here with a spare set of keys after our meeting." I said that I thought that it must seem to him as if his life depended on his making the phone call, but I thought that he and I should talk about what it was that was happening between us before attempting to undo it. [p. 178]

I think this is a key statement in this case example. Ogden gently directs the patient to the analysis and understanding of meanings and away from action that aims to suppress deeper meanings. The patient's proposed action would have been a repetition of past defensive actions and in this case it might have been ineffectual and certainly would have deflected away from the analysis. The patient responds to this intervention and shows a settling of his panic.

Ogden continues to explore these feelings with the man as his anxiety settles and he is able to focus on the event with the perspective of understanding that Ogden is offering.

Ogden demonstrates several important ways in which he translates his stance into the first-session activity. His emphasis is on the patient and anything the patient produces that has some as yet hidden meaning. From his statements about what he does in the first session and his synopsis of a first session we can see that he places the patient's productions before any demands or needs of his own as therapist. Ogden's perspective is that the first session is a session of analysis; there is no difference because it is the beginning. The analyst and the analysand enter these roles at the outset and both must begin their task. Therapy begins at the first moment. If not, an expectation for something other than an analytic process is initiated.

Ogden's primary objective in psychoanalytic therapy is to discover the meanings that words, feelings, actions, and experiences have for that person. This requires a particular type of space, the analytic environment. His interaction with the patient described above shows the way he begins to create this space for finding meaning and the way he involves the patient in this wondering and puzzling about meanings. The most poignant interaction with this patient involves the lost keys. Ogden does not forbid the patient's use of his phone as he might if he were simply following analytic rules, but he gently and spontaneously incorporates the patient's impulses and anxieties into the analytic process. He does not make the analytic encounter unsafe, which might occur with a prohibition of using the phone or with a failed empathy for the patient's panic; rather he engages the patient in the process of searching. Even at this early moment of the treatment Ogden invites the patient to consider what is going on between him and the therapist. The patient has already shown his sensitivity to authority in his recollection of a harsh father and early fantasies about what the therapist will require of him. Ogden recognizes the beginning of a repetition and interrupts it by acting in a nonauthoritative manner, inviting analysis, rather than encouraging a new enactment in the phone call. He surprises the patient in the midst of a reenactment and guides that surprise to the possibility of greater understanding. This patient responds well to the empathic and educative intervention and begins to unfold a more detailed story of his thoughts and fantasies in this moment.

The Patient as Self-Healer—Joel Shor

Shor's (1992) stance toward the patient arises out of a commitment to humanism and to a philosophy that holds that the process of analysis is intended to stimulate and advance the patient's self repair. He sees the task of the analytic therapist as being to "mainly facilitate the patient's attending to his own hidden values and reflecting on his private ways of making judgments and decisions" (p. 3). This task must "aim to avoid all pressuring to persuade the client to any moral position" (p. 3). He provides a description of his actual method for beginning an analytic therapy.

> However a patient initiates our contact, I have in mind a basic sequence of tasks for me as potential therapist: first, explicit negotiating on *all* practical matters of the process; next, offering empathic comment on signs of ill ease in negotiating and then presenting his complaints and wishes; and finally, when invited, making psychodynamic and transference interpretations. This sequence is renewed whenever the patient shows uneasy feelings. [p. 57]

For each matter of choice, beginning with a meeting time, Shor invites the patient to express his wishes. He demonstrates to the patient that "his choice is the first consideration" (p. 57). As this approach stirs anxieties in the patient or causes the patient to dismiss the choice, Shor has a point of entry into negotiation of the choice and consideration of the meaning of this experience for the patient. Shor shows his own flexibility about some matters and the places in which he is limited. But his intention is "from the start, he can see me becoming specially alert to both his preferences and to any signs of discomfort about asserting an easy self-directing manner" (pp. 57–58).

He continues:

> I aim to set a tone which suggests he may view our sessions as his time, his space, to explore whatever he may wish, and at his pace. My seemingly passive stance yet permits me to demonstrate that I can and intend to take care of my own autonomy and will try to be available to meet his explicit inquiries and his invitations to offer my best understandings as tentative hypotheses. A spirit of dialogue is offered, even as I sense his doubts and his demands for *my* leading the way. [p. 59]

A variety of themes about the therapist's stance are vividly illustrated by Shor's (1992) description of his beginnings with a patient. His primary concern is the patient's autonomy in conducting the treatment and discovering his hidden values and motivations. Shor translates this theoretical position at times by explicit explanation to the patient and by careful, empathic following of the patient's discomforts, to which he offers further explanation and interpretation when the patient is ready. A clear emphasis in Shor's work is the autonomy of the patient and of the therapist. As therapist he quietly insists upon his own autonomy and limitations and this is demonstrated to the patient each time the interaction between patient and therapist calls for it. He recognizes the constraints on both therapist and patient and willingly discusses this experience with the patient. Shor creates an experience that repeatedly illustrates the values he holds with a view to ultimately allowing the patient to find a freer expression of his own autonomy and a more conscious grasp of his own values. He holds Freud's position that all details of the therapy are left to the patient, and only takes a position of explaining and interpreting the patient's presentations as the patient wishes, or, in later phases of treatment, as transference distortions or threats to the therapeutic alliance emerge. Shor places great importance on the process of negotiation between therapist and patient, an interaction not so emphasized in traditional techniques. This acknowledges the two-person interaction from which the therapist draws the data that go into his assessment, empathic intervention, and interpretation of the transference relationship.

The Universal Symptom: Duplicity—Hellmuth Kaiser

Kaiser (1965) presented a theoretical point of view that some felt made him a renegade from psychoanalysis. He demonstrates his stance in a hypothetical first-session transcript. The session is lengthy and deserves attention as a whole, so it is not reproduced here. Kaiser asserted that, to be effective, psychotherapy must be an authentic communication between the patient and the therapist. He said that the universal symptom presented in psychotherapy was that of duplicity, an incongruence between feelings and words, and he presents his views in the form of a play about a series of early sessions. Kaiser's unique point of view is immediately evident in that the therapist plays the role of patient in order to treat the identified patient. That is, the therapist in the play is hired by the wife of a psychiatrist to make an appointment with her husband, as if the therapist were a patient seeking treatment, and to then initiate treatment without her husband's awareness, owing to the hopelessness she feels about her husband ever realizing his need. The doctor agrees. Even in this environment, in which the therapist is stripped of all authority and power to manage the session, he begins treatment.

Kaiser clearly rejects both rigidity of technique and the authority of the therapist as the fulcrum of therapy. He believes that success is best reached when the two individuals in the consulting room are able to communicate genuinely and intimately, and that such communication is rare and only effected with effort. His stance so completely saturates his communication with the patient that the defining roles of the therapy situation become secondary to the ultimate goals of the therapy.

Kaiser's (1965) stance de-emphasizes traditional techniques to such an extent that he can depict both his theory and stance as devoid of the roles of psychotherapist and patient. His play inverts this relationship, and in doing so dismisses these roles as essential to the process of therapy and growth. This further emphasizes that therapy works through experience, not cognitive processes or educative efforts. Therapy relies on the patient's experience of the therapist in a relationship in which duplicities come into evidence and then may be unraveled between therapist and patient. This in turn implies an equality between patient and therapist, in that both are responsible for their actions as well as for the congruity of those actions and their internal experience. From this follows the responsibility of the therapist for self-reflection and self-understanding, both as a prerequisite and an ongoing responsibility.

A Playground for the Transference Neurosis— Sigmund Freud

Freud (1913) is intent on the patient developing a transference neurosis, an intensity of relationship in which all of the neurotic projections are aimed at the therapist. Most of Freud's first-session activities, or nonactivity, work toward this goal. All this must occur in a kind of playground, a safe place in which both patient and therapist remain cognizant of the nature of the work. The patient retains a sense that the doctor is there to help and that the feelings and experiences occur within the "playground." The first-session example that Freud gives us is the case commonly referred to as that of the "Rat Man."

He writes, "A youngish man of university education introduced himself to me with the statement that he had suffered from obsessions ever since his childhood, but with particular intensity for the last four years" (p. 296). Freud goes on to relate various symptoms described to him by this man, including compulsions to cut his throat with a razor and fears that something might happen to people close to him. The man told of his various prior treatments, none of which had been effective, except for a stay in a sanatorium during which time he had had regular sexual intercourse with an acquaintance. Freud gives a variety of other descriptors relevant to his entire case presentation. He goes on:

> He gave me the impression of being a clear-headed and shrewd person. When I asked him what it was that made him lay such stress upon telling me about his sexual life, he replied that that was what he knew about my theories. Actually, however, he had read none of my writings, except that a short time before he had been turning over the pages of one of my books and had come across the explanation of some curious verbal associations which had so much reminded him of some of his own "efforts of thought" in conjunction with his ideas that he had decided to put himself in my hands. [p. 297]

Freud describes the beginning of treatment this way: "The next day I made him pledge himself to submit to the one and only condition of the treatment—namely, to say everything that came into his head even if it was *unpleasant* to him, or seemed *unimportant* or *irrelevant* or *senseless*. I then gave him leave to

start his communications with any subject he pleased and he
began as follows . . ." (p. 297).

Freud then goes on to relate the details of the Rat Man's story,
which involves many compulsions and obsessions about sexuality
and violence. Freud follows his own rules in this case. He gets the
man talking and insists on the fundamental rule. He explores
briefly the man's knowledge of his theories, which at that time
Freud felt might be a deterrent to the development of the
transference. He has obviously made the assessment that the man
presents symptoms and dynamics that will be treatable by
psychoanalysis. Freud does not jump to conclusions or take
actions with respect to the man's suicidal ideas, but he must
believe that they will be best addressed within the analysis. Freud
will then use the intensity of this man's fantasies and the intensity
of the regular six-times-per-week meetings to bring the transference neurosis into focus.

The Holding Environment—D. W. Winnicott

Winnicott does not give an example of a first session. However,
his patient, Margaret Little, tells of her experience with Winnicott, thus giving us a glimpse into how he began. Little (1990)
was an analyst training in the same institute as Winnicott. This
prior knowledge may have had some impact on the treatment,
though it is a common duality for those in training.

"So," she says, "thirteen years after first seeking psychiatric
help, and now aged 48, I came to D. W. I cannot give as clear,
coherent, or detailed account of the time with him as I could
wish. I can only recount some of the things that happened" (p.
41). Little goes on to tell of her meetings with Winnicott prior
to entering analysis. These were "slight" as she puts it, but
involved observing him in the institute and hearing his presentations as well as being referred a child by him after she presented
her membership paper. Then she relates her first sessions:

> The preliminary interview with him was short, perhaps fifteen
> minutes. At no time did he take a formal history of any kind, but
> feeling his way, built up gradually his understanding of what was

troubling me and of my "heart's need" (George Eliot, *Mill on the Floss*). I made my sexual affair [something she described earlier in her book] an excuse of not pursing the analysis; he accepted this but said that he would keep the vacancy open for the time being and I could take it up later if I wished. It was not long before I went back to him, as I found the sexual relationship difficult.

The first session brought a repetition of the terror [this was a presenting symptom that she described earlier in her book in regard to other consultations]. I lay curled up tight, completely hidden under the blanket, unable to move or speak. D. W. was silent until the end of the hour, when he said only, "I don't *know*, but I have the feeling that you are shutting me out for some reason." This brought relief, for he could admit not knowing, and could allow contradiction if it came. Much later I realized that I had been shutting myself in, taking up the smallest possible amount of space and being as unobtrusive as I could, hiding in the womb, but not safe even there. [pp. 42–43]

Little goes on to describe her later experiences with Winnicott and the manner in which he contained her anxieties and allowed for the analysis and understanding of her inner world. An emphasis in Winnicott's work that one sees Little is trying to convey is the careful and powerful holding of the patient. Little expresses this in her reaction to his seemingly minute comment in her first session, "he could admit not knowing, and could allow contradiction if it came." Winnicott created a safe haven for Little and he did this without being authoritarian. For Little, it opened a greater understanding of her state of mind. From the first Winnicott allowed her to express herself and direct the course of the beginning of her analysis.

Resistance Analysis—Herbert Strean

Strean's (1988) stance highlights the patient's resistances. He writes: "Ever since psychotherapy has been recognized as a legitimate form of occupational endeavor, clinicians have been preoccupied with their clients' resistances" (p. ix). Even in the phone call he notes evident resistances and the pervasive ambivalence patients experience toward psychotherapy. Strean reviews many aspects of beginning resistances and means of handling them. He writes in a direct manner with extensive case material. Many common problems are considered under the concept of resistance, including the telephone call, the involuntary client, client requests for information about the therapist, client reluctance to give personal information, requests for advice, and difficulties around the ground rules of therapy. He then enumerates a variety of common mistakes therapists make as viewed from the concept of client resistance. Among his many examples he reports a case of a young married woman who consulted a therapist for marital difficulties and sexual problems. The patient began the treatment with a question about the therapist's training. This therapist responded with information about her credentials. The young woman expressed how impressive her training was and acknowledged that the therapist must be competent. She commited to treatment, but did not return.

The same patient later consulted another female therapist of similar background. The patient again queried about the therapist's qualifications, but the therapist engaged the patient in an exploration about her concerns rather than simply answering the question.

> After a moment of silence, Jill said with some irritation in her voice, "I'm evaluating you and wondering whether you are qualified to be my therapist." Ms. Q. responded, "Apparently you have your doubts about me?" Here Jill smiled and said, "You were highly recommended by my internist, but I do have a lot of nervousness when it comes to talking about my problems. I have a lot of sexual problems too, and I'm embarrassed to talk about them with someone who is as knowledgeable as you are. I feel very inadequate and very inferior when I'm in a therapist's office."
>
> Ms. Q. empathized with Jill's plight and said that Jill seemed to feel like a second-class citizen next to a superior human being like the therapist. On hearing this Jill was able to laugh and say that was the way she felt in most of her interpersonal relationships and particularly in her marriage. She went on to describe her earlier contact with Dr. R. who, according to Jill "made me feel so inadequate and so incompetent when she told me about

her impressive list of credentials. I felt that I could never work with somebody who had accomplished so much more than I have." [p. 125]

The patient returned to this therapist and continued in the treatment. Strean concludes:

The above case demonstrates that the best way a therapist can deal with a client's questions about the practitioner's qualifications is to view the questions as a sign of resistance and an expression of feeling vulnerable in the therapeutic situation. When clients are shown that behind their queries are concerns and doubts about treatment, usually they are able to explore these doubts and concerns with the therapist. [p. 125]

This is a presentation of a common resistance met with in the first session, in this case with a naive patient. The meaning of the resistance is found to be a fear of something that will occur in the therapy, one that simulates characteristics evident in other places in this person's life. The patient in this case felt similar feelings in her marriage and other relationships, and the immediate exploration of the patient's question, seen as a resistance by Strean, began to bring this theme into the initial session. The analysis of this resistance served to make the patient feel more at ease and gave the new therapist a chance to demonstrate an understanding of this young woman's fears. The term *resistance* has in my mind developed a connotation of judgment in the mental health profession and even in popular usage. However, Strean here understands it to be the patient's fears that arise out of the very problems for which she courageously is seeking help. Note that Strean does not simply recognize the resistance. In fact he makes the case that resistance is ubiquitous in the work of psychotherapy. He observes it and skillfully uses the experience of the patient to enter an analytic exploration, guided by his empathic connection with the patient.

Diagnosis Directs Treatment—Otto Kernberg

Kernberg (1984) does not provide a case example of the first session, but the systematic interview he employs as a starting point to treatment illustrates another analytic stance and stands in contrast to the above examples; it is more clearly a medical model. Kernberg is specific that his presentation of the structural interview is designed for the training of psychiatric residents and he makes reference to its use in clinics and hospitals, though he indicates that he uses the same approach in his own practice. This systematic interview follows a tradition of history taking and diagnosis preceding the actual initiation of treatment. Kernberg's innovation is that the interview moves in a cyclical manner around a set of anchoring symptoms. He feels this allows the interviewer to return to areas for further investigation, since the interview does not move in a linear gathering of data. The interviewer regularly makes use of confrontation and other therapeutic interventions, both to establish a diagnosis and to ready the patient for treatment.

I find this to illustrate a medical model in the sense that a diagnosis becomes an important first step in the initiation of treatment, and it guides the interviewer in determining the appropriate referral for treatment. Kernberg's approach is deeply rooted in analytic theory and develops a diagnostic picture of the patient that is thorough and particular to the individual. In clinics, hospitals, and even for the private practitioner—especially one who specializes in work with borderline and narcissistic disorders—this clearly has an important function. And for the patient, time is not lost pursuing some mode of treatment, such as a formal analysis, which is contraindicated.

ESSENTIALS OF THE THERAPIST'S STANCE

The writers cited above allow us a look at how they conduct a first session and how they present a stance that will define future sessions. Each has an individual style and a particular emphasis, defined by personal dynamics as well as theoretical position. As individual as each writer's stance is, and as deeply rooted in differing theoretical orientations, they all share certain essential qualities of an analytic stance.

The stance of the therapist is professional and expert. All of these writers approach the patient with expertise and profession-alism, yet they balance this skillful stance with a humanness, and with the respect that is necessary to draw a patient into an analytic relationship. Shor (1992) emphasizes the importance of the patient's autonomy and freedom and he persistently encour-ages the patient to exercise these attributes. Bruch (1974) echoes this and specifically calls for sensitivity to the patient's needs in a relationship of mutual effort at understanding. Kernberg's (1984) approach appears more intentionally clinical, but his questions and mode of inquiry are sensitive and respectful and he is always ready to make a helpful and sustaining intervention in the course of assessment.

The therapist immediately sets about the task of creating a safe environment for the patient. It is interesting that none of these writers address the issue of safety directly. Schafer (1983) notes this about Freud, that the atmosphere of safety was an inherent characteristic of the psychotherapy setting. Strean (1988) shows the results of creating a place safe enough so that the fear that generates resistances can be understood. His examples show how it becomes possible for the patient to remain in treatment with the therapist as the fears represented in resistance are analyzed and understood. Ogden (1989) addresses the fear that leads to enactment in such a way that the patient feels safe enough to begin an analytic exploration, one of self reflection instead of repetitive reenactment.

The therapist's attention is on the patient—what the patient has to say and what the patient's dynamics are. There is no effort to dismiss the patient's experience, normalize felt troubles, or direct the patient's attention to some other matter. Each of these therapists pays attention to the patient first and foremost. The therapists do not direct initial attention to schedule, fee, paper-work, or policies; they only direct the patient to the patient's concerns, in an analytic way.

The therapist recognizes that the analytic relationship and all the themes of transference and resistance are set in motion at the first communication, and is ready for the early presentation of transference. This readiness takes several perspectives. Ogden (1989) is aware of the way early communications foreshadow unconscious anxieties of the patient as cautionary tales and he takes each production of the patient as an invitation to discern meaning. Shor (1992) pays attention to negative transference and the threat it may pose to the alliance between therapist and patient. Strean (1988) awaits the inevitable emergence of resistances that could abort the beginning of treatment. Finally, Bruch (1974) asserts that attention to understanding the patient in a focused and empathic manner is the best protection against missteps in the first session.

It is months after our first session; Gregg has continued with therapy and is regularly meeting with me twice a week. We have talked at times about the possibility of making a transition to formal psychoanalysis, but Gregg hasn't yet decided to increase his sessions and he's still thinking about feelings stirred by the idea of lying on the couch. At one point as this transition comes up, Gregg associates back to his first session. He says, "The first statement you made to me kind of threw me. I understand better now where you were coming from, but then, I had to sit back and think a bit. I expected you to ask me why I was coming to therapy or to tell you about my family or something like you expect with a doctor. You know, what's wrong. But you said—go ahead with what was on my mind . . . if I had been honest about it . . ." Gregg pauses and I spontaneously say something that he understands to be an encouragement to continue, even though he seems to be hesitating out of embarrassment. "Funny," he says, "it still feels embarrassing today. I wasn't really thinking about the session right when you said that. Well, of course I could hear what you said and I think I said something about how I would tell you about myself. But that wasn't what was on my mind then. I'd been expecting that you'd ask me about my past so I was thinking back to some events in my life and some of the things I've told you about my relationship with my mother. As soon as I had the thought I quickly got my mind away from it. I was embarrassed that I might let you in on how many fantasies I had about my mother—you know, things I've told you by now—but then, just starting, I was jarred by

how many thoughts came to my mind. At that point my mind
went to a time we were on vacation . . ."

FIRST WORDS—DEMONSTRATING THE THERAPIST'S STANCE

Psychotherapy does not hinge on the magical use of a few words,
a perfect interpretation, or any other single action the therapist
might take. Some actions and words have clear underpinnings in
an analytic stance, while some impede the process of psychotherapy by taking on meanings that interfere with the progress of
the relationship. Without overvaluing a few words, the initial
words a therapist says to a patient might be examined as they
support the overall goals of the therapy. As I talked to colleagues
about their first words to a new patient I heard about the first
words therapists do not use, some humorous, some the result of
an earlier problem the therapist was trying not to repeat. For
example a colleague told me of an experience in internship. She
opened the session with the comment, "So, what brings you here
today?" The patient replied, "The bus." She never started with
those words again. Another colleague told me that he always asks
a new patient how she would like to be addressed. He had
greeted a new patient, a young female physician who had
recently earned her M.D., by her first name, by which she was so
offended that she did not continue with him in therapy. She
aided his development of a more careful, empathic greeting to
new patients.

I want to examine a variety of first statements made by a wide
range of therapists. What follows are examples of the kinds of
openings many therapists use. However, the examination of first
words must not imply that there is a right thing to say. Analytic
therapists will always debate what the therapist says, how an
interpretation is formed, and the many uses of words. Freud's
(1913) statement about the "plasticity of all mental processes"
(p. 342) and the variety of presentations patients make applies
here. Therapists differ widely in style and in their ability to use
their unconscious and conscious characteristics. Many things are

said by therapists; some are accurate interpretations, some are nonanalytic statements and interventions, some border on destructive or useless, and some are antianalytic. But the ultimate failure or success of a therapy rests on the overall stance of the therapist, not just one statement. An examination of first words is intended only to apply the previous issues of stance to a more detailed aspect of beginning. I hope this may be a playful analogy to the broader exploration of the first session.

To Speak or Not to Speak

There is a notion among students who are beginning to learn to practice psychotherapy that analysts begin sessions without speaking. Perhaps the layperson believes that the analyst never says anything! The value of silence to the analytic process has been discussed in many places and ridiculed in just as many. The primary value of silence is to allow the development and verbalization of the patient's fantasy and thought processes. At times silence is used to create an optimal frustration to the patient's impulses for gratification from the therapist. The failure of gratification tends to keep the energy of the impulse active for production of fantasy and presentation of unconscious derivative material into the therapy. And sometimes silence is an empathic openness to the patient's need to be free of pressure. All of this is important over the course of psychotherapy and the use of silence is an understandable means of encouraging the process.

Many individuals, especially those treated in psychotherapy today, have personality dynamics that incline them to experience silence as distancing, isolating, overwhelmingly frustrating, and more of an impediment to the therapy than a help to association. At the least, the naive patient is more likely to be surprised by the therapist's silences in the first session. I do not think that silence as a typical opening is useful or recommended. While the patient's tolerance of anxiety and motivation for treatment must be assessed from the beginning, a few words at the start of the first session are of great value. Of course not all patients require the therapist's immediate opening, but there are several reasons why it may be a valuable consideration for most. For example, if the patient is naive to psychotherapy, the idea of a well-framed time period may be unexpected. Thomä and Kächele (1994) point out that in the health system in which they work, patients are typically referred by physicians. The patients referred have experienced meeting their doctor for a brief, undetermined time period. Such patients may have little expectation of meeting a therapist for an extended time period in which a significant development of their problems and complaints may be made. I think it worthwhile for the therapist to note the amount of time that will be available, allowing the patient to organize her thoughts without the added anxiety that the session will be cut off at some crucial moment. Thomä and Kächele note that this anxiety can place added stress on the patient and in fact can obscure the anxieties the patient has come to present. In today's atmosphere of cost consciousness and efficiency it is more likely that the patient is expecting to be rushed through a session rather than having a defined period of time in which to communicate her troubles.

The matter of safety is also a factor in first words. I do not want the initial moment of meeting a patient to be experienced as any more frightening or anxiety producing than is necessary to the patient's entrance into the therapy. Why stimulate anxiety unnecessarily? It is the therapist's responsibility to establish the framework of therapy and to acknowledge what those boundaries are. At the first session a number of aspects of the frame come into play. The therapist must protect those limits or the patient may experience a distrust of the therapist's ability to manage the frame of the therapy. I believe the first words best come from the therapist, but with attention to what those words create in the experience of the patient for the future of the therapy.

Therapist Anxiety

Sometimes the therapist's anxiety propels the first words. Though ostensibly designed to ease the patient they are actually aimed to ease the therapist. These comments take the form of small talk or social comments, the kind one might make meeting any stranger for the first time. One might say: "Did you have any trouble finding my office?" or "How are you?" or "Pleased to meet you" or "You mentioned in your phone call that you have been feeling depressed," and so on. This is chitchat arising from anxiety. Since therapy will require some anxiety in the patient in order to move forward, it is best not to ease that anxiety too quickly. Therapy is a serious, professional relationship. At the very least the therapist does not want the patient to mistake the relationship for a social one. Probably, beginning the therapy with no comment at all is better than such offhand comments, which arise out of the therapist's anxiety.

Comments like this can also raise further problems, because the therapist has no way of knowing at such an early moment the meaning the patient might attach to such words, even if the meaning may only be attached unconsciously. If the therapist asks, "Did you have trouble finding my office?" we must wonder if the patient experiences the therapist as questioning her ability to find her way about in life. Or if the therapist says, "Pleased to meet you," does the patient feel that to be an invitation to cover up those parts of himself that he believes the therapist will find unpleasant to meet? When an analytic therapist hears herself making such offhand comments, it ought to be a signal for some self-analysis about the source of the words and the potential for misstatement to the patient.

Therapist Concerns First?

A more disturbing form of beginning places the therapist's needs and requirements before the patient's. Sometimes these interventions are not even made with words. Handing the patient a history or information form to fill out before the session, raising issues of fee, insurance coverage, or schedule, or otherwise directing attention away from the patient's thoughts as the session is entered falls into this category. Certainly all of these therapist matters must be handled in the first session, but not at the very first moment. I believe this gives a message that the therapist's needs come first and abound beyond the scope of the patient's. A patient who fills out a form before seeing the therapist begins to build fantasies that may not reach awareness and this is antithetical to the nature of analytic therapy.

The legal and paperwork requirements placed on therapists seem increasingly to press for presenting myriad issues to the patient even before the patient states his concerns. I have heard speakers insist that it is in the therapist's best interest to have signed contracts before the beginning of the first session that state the disclosure and consents. I believe this sets the therapy off in a poorly conceived direction, and that the analytic therapist may wish to resist that approach. It is in no way unethical to take up matters of contract and consent near the end of the first session after the patient has had some time to explain his wishes and needs.

Promises, Promises

Another type of miscommunication is therapist promises. Perhaps these are not first words, but they may be early interventions ostensibly aimed at soothing a frightened patient. However it was stated, I have had several patients report that a previous therapist had promised "to always be there" for the patient or "to never give up" on the patient, or some similar communication. These promises undoubtedly arose from the therapist's understanding or intuition that this patient was terrified of loss and abandonment. It is also possible that these patients have distorted some other communication by virtue of their fears and projections. However, the demand for such a promise arises often enough, and the effect of such miscommunication is grave. It is realistically not possible to always be there; therapists go on vacation, move out of town, retire, fail to get phone calls, and so on. Even if all of those things can be averted, therapists are human beings and someday they die. Such promises are not indicative of the analytic stance to analyze; rather they represent an attempt to soothe by sympathetic action, and the ramifications they entail for the future of the therapy are significant.

At one point in the midst of my own practice I had to make a significant geographic move that necessitated the referral or termination of most of my patients. My move was unforeseen at the time I began treating most of the people I left. One patient noted to me with characteristic sarcasm and truth that analysts should never move. I partly agree with her, but nonetheless the realities of my life involved moving. I have never promised a patient to always be there, but even so some patients felt I had implied a rootedness, and felt betrayed by my move. Such a response can only be worsened by an actual promise. It is also most likely that those patients who press a therapist for such a promise are the more disturbed individuals who cannot be satisfied by any conscious promise. These individuals require the growth that comes in therapy, not more promises that cannot be kept.

Subtle Directives

Many first words are directive in nature. For example, a therapist may begin the first session with a comment that directs the patient to speak of the issues, complaints, or reasons for seeking therapy. One might say something like: "What problems are you having?" or "Why are you seeking therapy at this time?" or "How can I help you?" Such comments direct the patient to the complaints that have prompted the consultation. They effectively set in motion an assessment process oriented to the person's complaints and are akin to a formal diagnostic interview or history taking. Freud (1913) made such comments, asking the patient to talk about what he already knew about himself. Kernberg's (1984) diagnostic interview begins with a similar query. First words such as these are not likely to be disruptive to the beginning of an analytic process; most patients are ready for such a question, and find it calming to their initial anxieties. Such comments show that the therapist is interested and intent on getting to the point of the therapy. These openings also relieve anxiety about how the patient will begin. Many patients are probably used to such a routine from seeing medical doctors, who quickly seek to understand the current complaint. But they also place the therapist in the position of questioner or examiner, one who will direct the flow of the therapy, and from a knowledge of those complaints produce a treatment.

Good-Enough Ambiguity

"We will meet for forty-five minutes; I will let you go ahead with what's on your mind," is my opening sentence to a new patient, once we have come into the office and gotten seated. I will probably not open future sessions with a statement, leaving the invitation to "go ahead with whatever is on your mind" stand for all future sessions. This statement captures several factors I want to convey to the patient immediately. I want to define the time frame of the session. It is not endless, yet there is a substantial amount of time for the patient to develop a story about her meeting with me. The patient too anxious to ask about the amount of time will not have to talk as if we will only meet until I say so, which creates an unnecessary, even iatrogenic, anxiety in the first meeting. The time frame is in fact different from other professional meetings and will always be defined by some time limits in the future. And as the time of the session is set by me and guarded by me, I am able to take care of my own boundaries so that the patient can attend to hers. I do not ask a question here nor do I point to the patient's reasons for coming to me. I do not want to imply that the patient is unable to formulate a way of telling me what she has come for or that she is unable to recognize the purpose of the meeting. I do not want to direct or show interest in one thing or another. I want the patient to feel freedom to use the session however she wishes and, as in all future sessions, I want her to speak about what is on her mind at the moment the session starts. I intend to demonstrate right from the outset the nature of analytic therapy. It is a therapy that is focused on the immediate productions of one's mind and emotions. It is not focused on problems to be solved, but on freeing a person's development to independently solve problems.

Consider how a person might respond to this statement. Often enough a patient will begin by talking about the reasons he has come to therapy. That is a worthy beginning, likely what is consciously on his mind at that moment. Sometimes a person begins by asking about the fee and how long therapy will take. This immediately points to a variety of anxieties and the urgency with which those anxieties press for soothing. Or a person may come in agitated and begin by talking about how much traffic impeded his coming to therapy or how hard it was to find parking. In many ways these more spontaneous beginnings provide far more immediate information about what is going on in this individual's mind as he comes to the first session than a prepared speech about presenting complaints.

Many opening statements by the therapist will obtain the same kind of information and patients who are agitated or anxious will reveal this no matter how the therapist begins. My main point is that as therapists we think and rethink all that we do with the patient. Sometimes our approach immediately meets a sore point in the patient. Early in my career I was referred a patient who had been injured at her work. She had seen numerous professionals before meeting with me. When I queried what happened that she was seeking psychotherapy, she responded, "Dammit, do I have to go through all that again?" meaning, of course, that she was going to refuse to answer my question. She was correct. I only needed to listen to whatever she had to say to begin to understand what was going on. She continued in treatment a long time and eventually I learned what happened to her and much more that was necessary for her to tell. Our first words as well as all other words deserve careful examination so that they are in accord with the goals we hope to reach in psychotherapy.

Chapter 3

The Contract— First Negotiations

G regg appeared for his first session as we had arranged on the telephone. I was ready for him and met him on time to invite him into my office. We had already made the first negotiations of our contract for therapy. By meeting as planned we both met the simple expectations of our first agreement, which set a foundation for the further, more detailed issues that need to be set between us. The additional details of our contract for psychotherapy will not arise for discussion until the near the end of the first session.

FIRST NEGOTIATIONS

The first session of psychotherapy is the time when the concrete aspects of the contract for therapy are most closely discussed. Referring to time and money, Freud (1913) noted that once the practical matters are set therapy can proceed. The contract for therapy, however, is a far more complex agreement than time and money, which may just be the most concrete issues onto which patient and therapist project their difficulties with contracts and negotiations. A properly set contract, made with an eye to regular consideration of new areas of negotiation of that agreement, will make for a better ongoing therapeutic alliance. These negotiations are also a valuable arena for assessment of the manner in which the patient relates to the therapist and how the transference will develop. Throughout this chapter and in other places in this book the term *contract* refers to the complex negotiations and communications that are involved in the agreement to pursue psychotherapy. When referring to the contract as a document, now increasingly required by boards and the courts, the term *written contract* is used.

Menninger (1958) first discussed these matters as the contract, drawing a parallel between the therapeutic relationship and commerce between any two parties. Gitelson (1962) used the term *compact*, and Langs (1989) turned therapists' attention to the importance of the frame of psychotherapy. Some therapists dislike the term contract because it has legal (and litigious) connotations. Popular ideas suggest that contracts are made to be broken. For example, I was once asked to sign a job contract with the comment, "You understand this isn't what really goes on between us; we have a gentleman's agreement that is different from what the contract says." An attorney friend said, "Never sign a contract with someone who says that. The attorney's job is to make a contract that will serve both parties appropriately, regardless of how complex." That is the idea of a contract: it is a real statement of an agreement that does not seek to do harm to either party, does not coerce either party, and is not intended to be broken.

A contract for psychotherapy is implicit, even if it is poorly conceived. Psychotherapy is a part of contemporary commerce. Even though we provide a treatment that is empathic, humane, and intimate, we provide it for a fee as a professional service. Psychotherapy is not offered casually and is best performed with strangers. Freud (1913) noted early on that if one chose to analyze a friend, that therapist must be prepared to lose the friendship. Contrary to some patients' idea that psychotherapy is paid friendship, it is not. It is the skilled handling of the process of a relationship for the purposes of understanding and relief of suffering. While many forms of relationship may be analogous to the experiences in psychotherapy, such as confession, dependency, erotic longings, and friendship, psychotherapy is more than all of these. It is also provided professionally as a means of obtaining income for the therapist. Psychotherapy in our society is a part of commerce, it is a business, and it rightly involves a contract between patient and therapist.

The contract for psychotherapy is important beyond the arrangement of professional services. It is the beginning acknowledgment of all of the issues of boundary between the two people engaging in the therapeutic alliance. Understanding that the contract must be set in a direct and clear manner will set a stage for future negotiations of the transference relationship and avert a wide range of difficulties that might occur later on when previously unspoken expectations surface. At the same time, the negotiation of the contract provides the therapist with assessments about how the patient engages in relationships and what areas of ego boundary are strong or damaged.

Whether the therapist's stance is authoritarian or flexible, a contract must still be arranged. The therapist with a highly structured schedule and system of conducting treatment must still offer some suitable time to a potential patient for therapy to begin with that patient; otherwise the negotiations go no further. Flexibility in approaching a new patient is the preferable approach, and more likely to help an individual begin to talk about the fears and anxieties of beginning treatment. Given even a small amount of information, therapists can conjecture at length about a person's resistances to treatment, but the person can only be helped to understand those fears and resistances if he can begin the therapy. Similarly, even the most anxious person seeking treatment must at the very least be willing to make the phone call and meet the therapist; otherwise therapy cannot begin. Both therapist and patient bear responsibility for the establishment of an adequate contract.

Contract is a good term for this professional business agreement. But all relationships, even the most intimate, have agreements that are necessitated by the separateness of individuals and their boundaries. One of the reasons people seek psychotherapy is that these agreements run amok due to all manner of unconscious fears and wishes. In psychotherapy there is a continual goal of making these experiences conscious, and this is best done when the most concrete and necessary elements are acknowledged from the outset. Therapists struggle with these issues of therapy, time arrangements, and fees. But as much anxiety as these concrete issues present, they are probably simpler than those that will arise over the course of a long relationship with a patient.

Freud (1913) admonished therapists to address the practicalities of time and money directly. Even though he made much of the meanings of these issues in later work in the treatment, he emphasized the necessity of addressing them realistically and directly at the outset. The therapist who fears to confront these issues conveys that some things may go unspoken, a message that is antithetical to the process of the treatment. Freud warns us of the patient who wishes to place the discussion of these matters outside of the therapy session, as if they are the doctor's concerns and not a part of the treatment. But like all other matters and associations, the negotiations of time and fee must occur in the treatment; otherwise they may become something unspoken. Freud goes further; because he was writing to physicians beginning to practice psychoanalysis for the first time and who were changing from traditional relationships with their patients, he needed to change their stance. His admonition is important because it shows how a contract entered into with duplicity impedes the treatment. He charged the physicians with acting like generous philanthropists and then complaining in private at the lack of payments from patients. Understanding transference and the unconscious resentments that might hinder the therapist's work, Freud decried this practice and tried to teach a new stance, one in which the contract is made clear, so that the therapist's needs, introduced by the therapist, cannot intrude on the treatment unaware.

Other professional contracts are not part of the treatment. The surgeon will perform the operation without attention to his or the patient's feelings even if a third party collects the fee. Medical offices have all levels of billing personnel to handle these details so that the surgeon can get on with the treatment. But no part of the therapist's work can be successfully left out of the treatment. That is Freud's point, and it remains a valuable point today. Child and adolescent therapists often have additional difficulties in their treatment because the fee is necessarily paid by a third party and troubles arise from this situation.

There is a further benefit to the patient when the therapist negotiates directly. Naive patients may not understand why the therapist discusses and arranges the payments and schedules this way. Some patients feel that this takes up their time with matters that are the therapist's concern. However, the therapist knows that the contract is essential to setting the boundaries of therapy, that through these negotiations the therapist will be able to make an assessment of a good deal of the patient's process of interacting and managing anxiety, and that these aspects of the therapy will not be accepted by the patient for some time. The patient is most likely used to the physician's office, where he is guided through the process of payment and scheduling by a team of receptionists, office managers, and other support staff. The patient is unfamiliar with the therapist's ways and does not readily recognize that in the simple matter of costs the therapist has far less overhead than the physician by dealing directly with the patient. If every therapist had a team of office support staff, each session of psychotherapy would be much more expensive. More important, the therapist and patient would miss an opportunity for experiencing an essential part of the therapy, the creation of an agreement.

The Environment

The environment in which therapy occurs is also a part of the contract. It must occur in some specific space. Freud (1914b) first spoke of the playground of transference, an idea that Winnicott (1971) later elaborated. It is a critical concept and one closely related to the contract or frame of psychotherapy. A *playground* is a defined space usually with a fence or some other means of keeping the playing persons safe from what is outside, although I have noticed some playgrounds with fences seemingly designed to keep children out rather than in. Hopefully, psychotherapists do not create such spaces but seek to make inviting playgrounds. This playground has some important characteristics that must be anticipated in the contract. Schafer (1983) emphasizes the safety of the therapeutic space and discusses at length the qualities in the therapist's attitude that make for a safe environment in which the transference might grow and become a tool for the patient. The therapist seeks to allow the patient freedom to move about in the interior of her mind and fantasy. The fence around a playground is part of what makes these activities possible. Metaphorically, it excludes many items Freud first mentioned: prior contact between therapist and patient, other contacts outside the therapy space, and treatment of relatives. The contract will also cover how the therapy is conducted, including who does what: whether the therapist answers questions, makes recommendations, or enters the patient's life outside the therapy, and even the agreement to enter the patient's life *in* the therapy. This is a discussion of where the boundaries of the treatment stand, in the consulting room or beyond, how this affects the treatment, and how to arrange an agreement that meets the needs of two parties and best allows for the accepted process of psychoanalytic therapy. This negotiation foreshadows the more complex aspects boundaries present, and that involves the personal boundaries that are tried and studied in later, more intricate analysis of the transference.

Since the session has gone well and Gregg has agreed that he'd like to meet for a second session, I invite him to meet with me again the same week. I offer a time on Thursday, two days away. Gregg replies, "Oh, that soon. I was expecting . . . well, I don't know what. I guess some friends of mine who have seen a therapist went in once a week or maybe twice a month. I guess I was expecting that. But actually now that you mention meeting so soon it feels good; I've just gotten started and already I can think of more that I want to say." I say to Gregg, "It seems you recognize a disparity between what you've been told or even what you were expecting and the immediate experience you've had here. Maybe you can already see some contrast between your experience and all of the information you have in your mind." I leave it there, a tentative interpretation and a very beginning one, hopefully just enough to intrigue Gregg about his experience in the session. He says, "Yeah, I would like to come back on Thursday—that does feel good." I note to myself a bit of exaggerated enthusiasm, maybe covering some compliance. Gregg then goes on, "But I don't know about doing that for long—two times in one week—the money and all, and . . . uh, well—Does that mean you think I'm really in trouble?"

TIME

The Schedule

Time is a critical and persistent experience in psychotherapy. Patients and therapists have all manner of experience of time and later in the therapy these experiences can be used to great advantage in the understanding of transference. Time is first met in scheduling a first session. There will be no first session if a time cannot be arranged and there will be no therapy if no first session is arranged. These are not just practical matters that affect the flow of associations, but critical, concrete questions that must be settled. The deeply felt meanings of time for the patient can only be analyzed and understood if therapy proceeds. In contemporary therapy, setting the time for the first appointment usually takes place over the phone. This initial interaction about scheduling begins to give the therapist an assessment of the potential patient. For example, I have noticed patients asking for weekend and late-evening appointments, often due to the pressure of professional work schedules. The very request for such an unusual time is an indication of some resistance or hope for collusion by the therapist to accommodate the person's overly demanding work style. Scheduling must fit the lives of both the patient and the therapist, and the difficulties of making those arrangements begins the assessment of the potential patient.

Scheduling matters then persist throughout the therapy, even when the therapist seemingly sets a time that is never to be changed. After the first session is scheduled a second will have to be scheduled, and soon after that most therapists seek to arrange a set schedule for sessions. Even in that case the demands of contemporary living require changes at times in the regular schedule. Freud's (1913) practice was to lease the hour, for which the patient was responsible whether or not he attended the session. This undoubtedly reflected the practices of other professionals of the day; Freud used the analogy of the music instructor. Our society has changed and no doubt even music instructors schedule differently today. A certain consistency of meeting remains important to psychotherapy, but the practice of setting a time that is leased and will never change seems an overidentification with Freud's practice and fails to acknowledge the expectations of patients and the demands of a differently paced world. All of this is obvious and for most therapists a matter of course. Each therapist has a personal style and expectations about scheduling and the manner in which changes might be handled. But no matter what approach one takes, the first-session concern is that the way scheduling is handled will be a message to the patient, and the patient's approach to the issue will be an opportunity for early assessment by the therapist. This is a time when the limitations of therapist and patient meet, and perhaps collide. Patients have an opportunity to demonstrate their ready compliance, their early resistance to the process, their obsessive indecision, their feelings of urgency or failure to recognize urgency, and so on. A simple matter of commerce between two people becomes another piece of useful information. No doubt many therapists have had occasion to note to the patient that her reluctance to commit to some second meeting time may be an indication of fears or reluctance to engage in treatment. This is an early, tentative interpretation aimed at encouraging self-reflection, attempting to understand the resistance and make the decision to enter therapy possible, an assessment of what this person will do with an interpretation, and an educative demonstration of how the therapist will be thinking about their interactions.

Session Length

The length of a session is arbitrary. The recent popularity of the forty-five-minute session is evidence of its arbitrariness, a change from what for so long had been the standard fifty-minute hour and before that a sixty-minute hour. Free association does not require fifty minutes; we simply act upon a tradition and the demands of our present lives. It is most likely that the therapist's usual practice will dictate the length of the session although even Freud (1913) discussed adjusting the length of the session for some patients and Winnicott (Little 1990) extended the length of Little's sessions over her entire analysis. It is more likely that the length of time spent for the first session will be governed by the therapist. Adjusting the length of later sessions will occur in some negotiation with the patient when the patient's needs and the therapist's willingness are assessed. Some writers, in particular Kernberg (1984) and Bruch (1974), have a practice of making the first session longer than later sessions, extending to sixty or one hundred twenty minutes, to allow time for all the demands of this first meeting. The value of this approach is obvious, since there is a great deal to accomplish in the first session. However, the effect of creating an expectation by extending the first session must be considered. If that approach is taken it must be made clear to the patient.

Every session is unfinished. How often we hear patients say "This wasn't long enough," or "I have more to say," or "You always stop me just when I'm starting to open up." The first session will also be unfinished; it is, of course, the beginning of a long time together if the decision is made to continue. If the business of setting the contract in its most basic form is unfinished another session can be offered soon after the first to continue the patent's story and complete the basics of the contract. The nature of the therapy is again demonstrated. Session time is limited, a continuity will have to be developed over time, and the patient's story and the growth of the relationship with the therapist are endless. But there may be reasons to extend a first session without prior arrangement. When confronted by an acutely distressed patient who may require additional containment, referral, or even hospitalization, the demonstration of the limits of the session may have to give way to good ethics and sound judgment in attending to the patient's welfare. Obviously there are always reasons to set the guidelines aside in emergencies and unusual circumstances. But in the usual course of events there is good reason to create clear indications of what will occur in future sessions.

I use the term *session* when I speak with patients, though the word "hour" is common and I have used it in the past. I changed my wording because many patients took the word "hour" literally, something that is only hard to understand when we fail to consider the use of our own jargon and the confusion it may create. Several people became perturbed when the hour ended fifteen minutes short, since I had always met for a forty-five-minute session. This example highlights the importance of our terms and the careful use of words in our work. Actually I mean not only the careful use of words, but the constant search for meaning, the recognition that words take on different meanings, and finally that the work of analysis is elucidating these meanings and keeping them straight in the analytic dyad.

Frequency

Of all therapies, analytic therapy has emphasized the value of frequent meetings in order to enhance the intensity of the treatment and the depth of the transference. The strongest and most common argument for a frequency of more than one meeting per week relates to the material a patient might reach in the time available. A person's day-to-day experiences are clearly a great part of the material that is presented in sessions, and infrequent meetings are often taken up with necessary explanation of such events in the patient's life. More frequent sessions allow for the development of the therapist–patient relationship and the many feelings and experiences that make for transference observations. While some patients may use infrequent sessions to great advantage, developing a strong relationship to the therapist, most do not and benefit much more from more frequent meetings.

The experienced patient is often aware of the value of frequency and may even request therapy with a readiness for two, three, or more meetings weekly. The knowledgeable patient seeking formal psychoanalysis is most likely aware of the tradition of four or five weekly meetings and comes with an expectation of this availability from the therapist. But many patients are naive to therapy and must be educated by experience and information if they are to meet more often than their initial expectation. As therapy has gained wider public attention, I find that most patients expect to be seen at least once per week, though the request for monthly meetings is not unknown. Exploration of the request often reveals conscious fears about the cost of therapy and the patient's attempts to make the treatment affordable. Much has been written about the further unconscious motives and fears evident in the desire for infrequent meetings, and this immediately becomes material for exploration and a chance for the therapist to demonstrate the nature of analytic therapy. I think it interesting that once-per-week therapy has become so expected by patients. Since psychoanalysis with meetings of four to six sessions per week has been a model of psychotherapy, I wonder how the frequency of meetings was so diminished. No doubt the influence of insurance reimbursement has had a grave effect on the public's thinking. Unfortunately, therapists seem to have taken up this notion as well. If the insurance industry continues to have this effect we may find that six sessions in a year becomes the expectation, once every other month therapy!

Length of Treatment

The question of how long treatment will take is an unwelcome one for all therapists and it often arises in the first session. Even Freud (1913) felt this discomfort and offered some supervisory comments to therapists as to how it might be answered. This is a complicated issue. The therapist does not wish to give the impression that unknowns can be answered with authority. Since more extensive assessment will have to take place and since the question of length of treatment varies for each patient, there is no simple answer. But the therapist also does not like to respond so vaguely as to be experienced as deflecting the patient's questions at this early stage of treatment. After some experience together, therapist and patient will develop a mutuality about the nature and success of treatment and the appropriate end point. This

question, like all others, may also be an invitation for exploration
and analysis. Yet the question itself may be a pressing one that
requires some concrete response. Many naive patients will feel
put off if a more concrete answer is not given.

Most patients are not asking about the clinical theory of analytic therapy. Rather, they are anxious about the beginning of a
serious endeavor and the resolution of some problem or anxiety.
An explicit statement about the long-term nature of analytic
therapy might frighten a new patient, stirring up fantasies that
might never be open to analysis if the person leaves in resistance
to what the therapist has predicted. I saw a woman once who was
referred early in my analytic training by a member of the faculty
of my institute. The referral was made with the note that this
might be a good training case. I then imagined a four-time-per-
week treatment with a willing patient who I also imagined had
been more fully assessed by the referring psychologist. When the
patient asked the usual questions about treatment length and
frequency I quickly returned with an offer of analysis. I failed to
adequately assess the patient's present state of mind, openness to
treatment, or knowledge of therapy. She showed conscious
interest in my description of analysis, but clearly was frightened
by the prospect of what I was proposing and did not return. This
was the error of a novice, and an enthusiastic one to be sure; I
moved on the basis of my deference to a senior colleague and
failed to follow and understand the experience of the patient. In
contrast, a colleague tells me that his first experience of analytic
therapy was greatly enhanced by the therapist's commitment to
the frequency. In the initial meeting the therapist directly
indicated the necessity of twice-per-week therapy. The patient
reeled at first, fearing an inability to pay for the treatment. With
further consideration he realized that this therapist believed that
something could happen in therapy. He was moved by a hopefulness that other therapists had not instilled in him. Here, the
assessment of the patient and timing of the response about
length of treatment or frequency was crucial to making the
hoped-for impact.

A colleague gives this answer to the question of "How long?"
He says that the length of treatment cannot be predicted with

confidence, but the following is his experience with psycho-therapy patients. Those who stay in treatment six months and beyond seem to report the greatest benefit. Those who stay less than six months seem to gain less but, nonetheless, can feel some benefit. I find this an interesting way to give some sense of a time frame to the direct portion of the patient's question. It is a way of saying, "Try to stay about six months." I imagine this does several things for the patient. Most reasonable people would not see six months as intolerably long for the sort of question one brings to a psychotherapist. It is not a frightening length of time. The therapist knows that the question cannot be addressed fully at this point, but if given time to experience the relationship of therapy, after six months or so the patient may be able to discuss this question in an entirely different manner if it ever arises again. This provides a sufficient, honest answer to the conscious question of a naive patient. It is relieving enough of anxiety to allow the patient to go on, and the deeper questions may be dealt with at a later stage when the treatment alliance is better formed and some experience of the analytic process has occurred. It is likely that even early patients of analysis did know the time frame for a "completed" therapy, even though Freud's answer did not state a time, as it was known then that analysis took from about six months to a year.

Asking the question about treatment length is probably more interesting than the answer the therapist gives to the question. One could say, leave any time you wish, although some would simply not believe the therapist. Or the compliant patient might unconsciously fear getting stuck with demands of the therapist. The question from the patient is another entry into the analysis, an exploration of the anxieties, and a demonstration of how the analytic therapist proceeds. This may be a moment when the tactful therapist can elicit the patient's thoughts about the length of therapy or even her fears about it lasting too long or not long enough. The therapist may be able to gain some early sense of the themes in this patient's fears. Is the patient fearful of accommodating the therapist to the detriment of his own wishes, or is the patient perhaps defending against her dependency feelings, hoping for a short therapy when her unconscious seems

to press for dependency? The therapist's gentle, empathic encouragement to explore such questions and concerns demonstrates early on how the patient's experience will be used to gain
greater self-knowledge in an analytic way.

Endings

Beginnings are inevitably linked to endings. Patients express
concern about how long therapy will last, that is, a concern about
endings. But there are repeated endings in any therapy that
deserve some attention in the contract, most immediately the
ending of the session. The first crucial ending experienced by the
patient is the end of the first session. It must occur, whether it
occurs at the time specified in the initial contract for forty-five
minutes, or an hour for the initial consultation, or at some
unspecified time after the contracted ending because the patient
seemed to require more and the therapist found that to interrupt
the patient was too anxiety provoking. There is reason for the
therapist to consider establishing a longer first session, as Bruch
(1974) and Kernberg (1984) do, because so much must occur in
the first session. There is reason also to make the first session just
like all other sessions, emphasizing that therapy has begun and
will occur in other sessions just like this first one. Whatever one's
personal choice for first sessions is, the first session must end.
How it ends is another moment of assessment for both patient
and therapist. Some patients experience the end as an interrup-
tion, seemingly intolerable, to fantasies that the therapist will be
an all-good mother who is available to the patient's primitively
felt needs for attention and caring. This will occur again and
again if treatment proceeds. But the end, like all other boundaries, is a crucially important limit of the therapy, and a clear
demonstration by the therapist of those boundaries agreed to in
the first contact. It is a matter of the safety of the analytic setting.
Consider what the patient might experience if the therapist has
difficulty ending the session, if the therapist is anxious about
interrupting, or unempathic to the patient's sense of the abruptness. The therapist must be able to show an ability to manage the
boundaries of the therapy; this becomes particularly important

for those individuals who come to treatment with a history of failed parenting, violation, intrusion, and parents who were unable to offer protection. In the analytic situation we want to create a space in which the experience of availability and good-enough parenting can be felt and explored in all its depths, but we cannot create this in actuality. And we must also be able to manage the realities of adult life, where endings occur and limitations are experienced and managed. The first ending is the first demonstration of this. For the therapist, the way the patient approaches this first ending is another instance where the beginnings of the transference are presented. One patient will try to hang on to the therapist in the first session, increasing the intensity of his emotional tone as the end nears. Another patient will end her presentation with some minutes left on the clock, fearful of evidencing her neediness or of experiencing the coming felt rejection by the therapist. Some patients will react with frustration or anger that the time is so short, and so on. But the end must occur, and many more endings and beginnings will take place as therapy proceeds. Whatever one chooses as a time frame for the first session it is a valuable practice to end at the specified time. This is the best demonstration of the therapist's capability of protecting the therapy space, managing her own affairs (time for the next patient, a break before the next patient, or a return to personal concerns), and that therapy is a professional relationship that has limits. Further experience of endings will continue to occur in the treatment, including the end of the week, ending before vacation, and so on. These are all as pertinent to the psychotherapy as the beginning.

Chapter 4

The Contract— Fees and Legal Issues

I check the time as Gregg tells me his concerns and his reasons for seeking psychotherapy. While he's been talking I've been feeling interested in his concerns and certain that from what I've learned I could work with him. I'm willing to begin working out some details for continuing. I notice that it's just minutes before the end of the session, whereas I usually leave about ten minutes to deal with scheduling the next appointment and arranging a fee. Gregg has begun to feel more comfortable speaking about himself to me and I have gotten engrossed in his story. I reflect for a moment that I must think about why I lost track of the time, but I quell my concerns for now; I know that because I often run over in a first session I've left sufficient time before my next appointment. I find an appropriate pause to suggest that we consider some of the business matters. Gregg is jarred a bit by my words, perhaps feeling how absorbed he was with his story. I ask him if he wants to return for another session, and he agrees, but then he says, "Shouldn't I be coming for more than just another session?" I reply, "Yes, what you're talking about will certainly take more than two sessions to understand, but let's just take one step at a time. We're about out of time now, so maybe we could use some time in the next session to think about where you'd like to take this with me." Then I suggest we talk about the fee. I tell Gregg my fee is $125 per session. I wait to see his reaction and response, since I didn't hear any particular anxiety about finances as he talked. Gregg says that will be all right and that he thinks he has some insurance coverage he might want to use for his therapy. I suggest that he check into the insurance and we could consider together in the next session how to use it. As we move on to other matters, I'm relieved that Gregg agrees to the fee so easily. It reminds me of the many instances when new patients have had strong reactions to hearing my fee, or conflicts that immediately surface when the fee is discussed. I feel my own anxiety about the topic. I wonder if Gregg will discover more conflict in the future even though he seems to be taking the issue in stride at this juncture.

FEES

Psychotherapy is provided for a fee. This is an essential part of the contract and a part fraught with much difficulty. Eissler (1974) discussed many of the issues involved in the fee for psychoanalysis. He considered an exhaustive list of problems and concerns. The foremost issue for the first session is that a fee must be paid and the negotiation of payment of that fee is part of the therapy. The nature of psychotherapy allows the unconscious to project that the therapist is like a mother who does the work for love. Few other professionals experience such a powerful projection of this need. Therapists have their share of anxiety about charging the fee, even though obviously for the private therapist the fee is her livelihood. Problems for the therapist exist in charging too much and in charging too little, in collecting the fee, and in enforcing whatever agreement is made for changes in the schedule. All manner of important self-analysis may be generated by one's anxieties about charging a fee and interacting directly and clearly with the patient about this matter. Does the therapist devalue his services? Does he collude with a patient's devaluation? Is the fee felt to be punitive? Do personal financial strains and anxieties motivate an undue demand on the patient that impedes deliberate analysis and empathy toward the patient? These are some typical questions.

It is not in the scope of the first session to analyze all the possible meanings of the fee held by either the therapist or the patient. Even though the fee may be settled in the first session, associations and conflicts about it will continue to arise over the course of time. The fee is one of the most poignant areas where the therapist's needs and desires impinge upon the patient. Negotiation of the fee is another first-session matter, one in which all of the future work of analysis begins to be demonstrated to the patient. It is a point of considerable anxiety for the therapist and an area that too often stirs our defenses, impeding the work that is just beginning.

Usually the fee must be established in the first session. Sadly, I have found that licensing boards are codifying the very time at which a fee must be announced to the patient. For example, some therapists must state the fee over the telephone. Greenson (1967) reveals that he dislikes it when the question of the fee arises on the phone. He explains how he handles this. His point is not to lure the patient in unaware and then hard-sell the therapy, a picture the new ethics codes seem to anticipate. His effort is to get the best possible assessment of the patient before making any recommendations of treatment or any negotiation of the fee, if that person is going to continue in treatment. Obviously, it is unethical in any business to bring a person into a situation where a charge will be made without in some way alerting the person to the fact and the nature of the charge. But for the therapist, establishing a fee and an agreement to work together at whatever fee requires assessment, and usually this is best done in person. The struggle is to avoid being seductive, while drawing in potential patients who have no knowledge of the fee without frightening them away by raising resistances before some assessment can be made. Unfortunately, increasingly concrete ethics codes are limiting our judgment as professionals as to what action to take.

Cancellations—The Fine Print of the Contract

Analytic therapists have all manner of approaches and arrangements for dealing with missed sessions, and all manner of their

own resistances to the subject. The nature of the agreement
about missed sessions is naturally one of personal style and is not
as important as the manner in which it is reached and the
meanings attached to it. This is the "fine print" of the contract
because it is so easily overlooked or forgotten by the patient and
may cause a fair amount of conflict in the course of therapy. The
way canceled sessions are dealt with need not always be handled
in the first session, but they are part of the contract, and an
implicit expectation of the therapist. I have heard a variety of
arrangements for dealing with canceled and missed sessions. We
know that Freud leased the hour, with all sessions to be paid for
whether or not the patient arrived, arrived on time, or even
provided notice of cancellation. Freud is clear that the primary
purpose for this arrangement is the analyst's need to have some
certainty about his income and that his income not be subject to
the vagaries of the patient's resistances, which might be acted out
in cancellations or missed sessions. Many therapists continue to
require similar arrangements, with modifications around vacation times. Some have felt it not in their nature to require
payment for canceled sessions and recognize that any therapist
must expect some fluctuation in income, canceled sessions being
an expected part of conducting therapy as well as life. Some allow
for cancellation within a certain time frame, usually set by the
therapist, perhaps twenty-four or forty-eight hours. I have also
heard of more elaborate cancellation policies that involve no
charge if the session is rescheduled, or no charge if the therapist
is able to fill the hour with another paying client. If the therapist
has a strict policy for cancellation and payment, this most
reasonably should be clear to the patient at the outset of therapy
in the negotiation of the contract. A patient is rightly disturbed
if he is confronted with an unusual expectation by the therapist
after numerous sessions and when that expectation is non-
negotiable. A person's reaction of surprise at being charged for
the first canceled session is not a matter of negative transference,
but a reasonable reaction to a poorly presented expectation in the
contract for therapy. I find the more elaborate policies for
cancellation confusing and overly complicated. Understandably,
a therapist must make some provision for protecting his income,

but an overly complicated policy is confusing and then hard to enforce. Certainly a patient's ego mechanisms are affected by transference and resistance so that policies are forgotten and the usual expectations of professional relationships are altered. But an overly confusing policy for cancellation or any other matter may become a provocation of negative reactions and an unnecessary intrusion into the already complicated matter of transference.

Policies and Purposes

While a policy for patient and therapist that is comfortable and serviceable is a desirable end to the negotiation of the contract around cancellations, the further purposes of such a policy are worth considering. First is the therapist's comfort that income will be predictable from week to week and that seeking other activities to fill those sessions is not necessary. The therapist can concentrate on the therapy. But there are additional reasons for placing limitations on the cancellation of sessions. These matters are alluded to by Freud (1913) in regard to the influence of the patient's resistance. Resistances will arise and often enough are enacted at the point of attendance to agreed-upon therapy sessions. If only because some degree of frequency is desirable for the therapy and necessary for continuity, some understanding of the effect of cancellations must be worked through. In my work I tend to avoid standard policies about cancellation, and for that matter many other aspects of the contract. My preference is that all matters of the contract be worked out specific to the patient I am dealing with, recognizing that I have routines, some of which cannot be adjusted too far. I am willing, therefore, to discuss and if necessary creatively deal with unusual schedule demands, as for example with the traveling business person or the physician who must take calls. I try to deal with these issues as they arise, making the experience of what is going on much more presently available. Stating a cancellation policy to a new patient may be received by that patient in a variety of ways unknown to the therapist, even if the surface, conscious reaction is business-like and understanding. We do not know, and often in a first session do not have the means to know, what unconscious meaning this may have for the patient. Perhaps it stirs a feeling that the therapist does not trust his commitment to the therapy. The patient may not express a reaction to the cancellation policy at the time it is announced, but this may be because the experience of canceling a session is not within the patient's grasp at that moment. Certainly there is some value to arranging these matters early in the treatment. Their presentation is not a matter of a simple contract or listing of information for consent. We are engaging the patient's unconscious processes, and thus many meanings are at play besides the legal and ethical issues apparent in the negotiation of a contract.

I typically deal with cancellations as they arise in the hopes of conducting the therapy relationship in a manner as close as possible to that of a spontaneously evolving experience. I expect that anyone starting psychotherapy will at some future time need to cancel a session. But I do not invite cancellations by offering a cancellation policy. Sometimes it is many months before a very compliant patient will even broach the subject of cancellation and then all manner of important experiences arise around how long it took to ask, how much anxiety was involved in asking permission to cancel, and how many things might have been subordinated to the therapy session without even the possibility of considering the conflicts. Of course there are patients who are just the opposite, who cancel as if to show no regard for the therapy, and who insist even before the discussion begins that they will never pay for a canceled session. Here the transference issues are engaged in the moment and the work of therapy ensues. I enter this non-policy arrangement for cancellations with the understanding that I may not get paid for the first session that is canceled too closely to the time of the appointment for my comfort. I have not announced any preferences so I do not expect a patient to guess my wishes. I do expect a person to recognize the importance of his own responsibility for fulfilling the demands of his life, whether these are emergencies, business or family demands, or sickness. I do not hesitate to indicate to the person who misses a session without notice that I believe it is understandable that he be responsible for his slip of the mind or emergency that made it impossible to notify me. My wish is that any session be canceled at least a whole session before. I have never tried initiating this as a policy, but my intention would be that any cancellation be discussed with time to consider the meaning of the cancellation, a matter we too often ignore when we have a policy, and that the cancellation be directly negotiated between the two of us, with attention to the meanings in the therapy.

The therapist's limits are crucial to the process of therapy, and clarity about one's limits is essential. However, policies can cause us to miss meanings. Policies about cancellations reduce the very anxieties that might be experienced and used in the course of therapy as many experiences are enacted in the relationship. As I noted earlier, if the therapist's style is one of clarity and specificity regarding expectations for such issues as cancellation then I do believe that those expectations must be raised at the outset, especially as those demands differ from the routines of the community. For example, if a therapist expects cancellations one week prior to the session, this is divergent from general community practice and would be a shock to the patient who first cancels eight months into the therapy, unaware of the consequences. Handling policies this way is unfair and also risks complaint if the procedure is not made known at the outset. In my approach, the nature of the agreement will be negotiated at the time the need arises, and the patient is free to make extra demands on me. I have no specific policy except that each of us be responsible to the other and to the therapy.

First-Session Fees

I ran across the notion of not charging for the first session in an awkward moment with a new patient. We had moved through other parts of the first session, and upon discussing the business matters it was apparent that this woman had come with the expectation that therapists do not charge for first sessions. She was naive to therapy; she had seen one other therapist for one session, and that therapist ascribed to a policy of not charging for the first session. I was not aware of this practice and we had to negotiate together how to handle this misunderstanding, in which the patient felt particularly embarrassed. I have taken the position that I charge for my time, that the first session is no different than all later sessions, and that it is reasonable to expect payment for that time as well. I do not want to give the impression, consciously or unconsciously, that some of my time is provided differently than for a fee. Furthermore I believe that if a person is embarking on a project of analytic therapy the cost in fees over a significant period of time will probably make payment for one session negligible in the whole project. I particularly reject not charging for the first session as a marketing lure to new patients when the endeavor of psychotherapy is a serious and costly decision, the value of which cannot be judged by one meeting. So I have taken the position that my time is what is paid for and that the first session is just as expensive as the rest. However, some colleagues have challenged this.

The main reason for offering a free first consultation is the anxiety of the patient that therapy might not work out with this therapist. The patient in this case is assessing his fit with the therapist. In theory most therapists would agree that this is a good project and that it might even stir a bit of good analysis with any therapist consulted. In this case we allow the patient some latitude to make a self assessment in the course of selecting a therapist. This is an ability that we hope to encourage in psychoanalytic therapy and an area often found lacking in patients who seek treatment. So, if one chooses to offer a free first consultation, how might it be done? First of all, it cannot be done as a seduction. This is antithetical to analytic therapy and will quickly confound the transference. The therapist's personal treatment or self analysis offers the best means of understanding these impulses. A number of therapists to whom I have spoken offer a first consultation at no charge and this is communicated on the phone. A creative addition to this method is made by a colleague who offers the first session at no charge if the patient decides not to return. If therapy is continued, payment for the first session must be made, even if the person returns years later to resume treatment. This averts the problems of miscommunicating the value of the therapist's time and yet allows for the time needed by patients who are trying to make a reasonable determination about their fit with a therapist.

Setting the Fee

Setting the fee with a patient is a task that has been filled with anxiety and is the subject of much consideration in the literature. In my own work and in my work with therapists in supervision I have further confirmed the difficulties in this area, and yet setting the fee is essential to the work of psychotherapy. As Freud (1913) first noted, the therapist is responsible for handling matters of money in the same direct and open manner that will characterize the handling of all future matters. Again, the formation of the transference and the nature of the stance of the therapist all require that fee setting be handled directly, with no difference from the way other matters are handled. Otherwise the therapist has conveyed that some matters are too difficult to address and may be dismissed to an area of the unspoken. The topics to consider are: How does a therapist establish a fee even before discussing it with the patient? When and where in the first session (or phone call) is the fee introduced? Is the fee negotiable? How is it negotiated? Who "owns" the fee?

Setting one's fee is a somewhat arbitrary process, aside from the fee agreements made with insurance companies, Medicare, and managed-care contracts. I am describing here how to set fees for privately paying patients, those who are not involving a third-party payor. There is no true standard and no simple way to outline this process. One's fees clearly must be based on training and experience, the commonly charged rates in the community, and one's ability to attract potential patients to his practice. There is no use holding out for one's "full fee" if no referrals call who can afford that fee. There is a business aspect to setting one's fee that has to do with the demand for one's services. Clearly, any student of human personality recognizes that some will overvalue their services and some will undervalue them. This is something that cannot be taught. It is a matter of personal self understanding and personal ethics.

When is the fee set with the patient? If the therapist does not reduce her fee then there is no need to suggest in a phone call that the patient "talk about it" if that implies that the fee will be changed. There are many reasons and great value to talking about the fee, all of which are important material for the therapy. But the willingness to negotiate a reduced rate or not must be made clear. Ethics codes increasingly demand that fees be stated even as early as in the first phone contact. These codes are attempts to constrain those therapists who use deceptive practices, luring a patient into a process the patient cannot afford, or with hidden charges that surprise that patient at some point. Such practices are unethical and counter to the process of analytic therapy. One cannot conduct a process requiring openness and honesty and begin it deceptively, whether about the fee or any other matter.

Today, amid the growing concerns about ethics and laws affecting the therapist, I have heard lengthy talks about the honesty and ethics of various manipulations of fees charged to insurers. It is my opinion that it is hard to generate much concern for an industry that has manipulated therapists and their livelihoods without much apparent concern for ethics. However, the more important issue for the analytic therapist is the message conveyed to the patient by manipulation or dishonesty. One must question how these deceptions play into the transference and the call for honesty between the two individuals establishing a therapy relationship. Again, the basic concept is that the patient's unconscious does not overlook the therapist's actions.

The increasing demands on the therapist for concrete actions in the areas of disclosure and written contracts are disturbing because they tend to limit the many possible ways of entering into a relationship. Policies about how to set fees limit the therapist's observations and experience inherent in working out the fee with the patient. Whether or not one negotiates a fee, the process of discussing and arranging it offers many hints about the transference. These experiences and anxieties are best observed in a face-to-face session, not on the phone or as a patient reads a sheet of policies. My preference is to meet with all patients, regardless of their own perceived ability to pay, and then to explore the concerns about payment, the available resources, and any anxieties about the fee that might be addressed. If I choose to hold my fee at its full rate I state it at its full rate. I want to explore with the patient fantasies, expectations, and even the beginnings of negative transference. If I choose to reduce my fee I want that reduction to be for purposes of realistic considerations, following a careful review of the person's ability to pay. I do not believe that I can be the judge of someone's ability to pay. Individuals have all sorts of ways of determining the use of their money and I am not so arrogant as to believe that I can be the judge of how that ought to happen. Of course I value therapy and I wish to be paid for my services, so it is sometimes hard to see the other person's point of view.

Reducing Fees

Regarding the reduction of one's fee, several issues arise. One might, as Greenson (1967) did, refuse to have a set fee and work out the fee with each patient. Yet presumably even Greenson had some range in which he was willing to work. For the experienced therapist who has been successful in promoting her practice, it is probably most common to set a fee and hold to it as noted above. I would consider it odd that someone would try to get a reduction in fee from $150 to $135 per session. It hardly seems that such a reduction would make it more possible to continue in treatment. In these cases, no doubt, the request for fee reduction has some other meaning, one that a person is sometimes willing to consider within the analysis. For new therapists trying to build up hours in practice and develop skills and referral sources, I always suggest taking anyone who is interested, assuming that getting even a small percentage of one's fee is better than sitting in an empty office waiting for the phone to ring. Reductions are also made in training settings in which the therapy is provided by a trainee, and the supporting institution attempts to make therapy more widely available or is conducting research that requires some activity for the research from the patient.

When a patient appears for therapy and the fee required by the therapist is far from affordable, the person is clearly in the wrong office. Reducing one's fee in these cases seldom serves any good purpose unless the therapist is committed to pro bono work and chooses this patient for that service. I think that some exploration and analysis of how the patient got into such circumstances is advisable. Is this a matter of reality testing, poor judgment, some intellectual deficiency, or an expectation that therapy is done without compensation? One wonders why a person arrives in a therapist's office with little practical understanding of the costs. Perhaps a brief analysis of some of those issues with the patient will aid that person in making a better selection and connection with a therapist who can accept a significantly lower fee.

Once a therapist told to me that he "owned the fee." I think he was trying to say that it was not up to the patient to set the fee or demand negotiation with the therapist. I had never thought about the matter that way. I am more inclined to think about the fee as something both therapist and patient own, in the sense that it is agreed upon in a noncoercive negotiation. What I think this therapist was trying to assert is that the fee is something within the scope of his limits and his personal expectations in the therapy. I think he was trying to protect the negotiation from stretching his boundaries. It is important that the therapist enter into an arrangement that is comfortable, because undue caretaking of a patient by reducing a fee will make for a troubled countertransference reaction in later stages of the therapy as well as unconscious transference expectations of the patient being given special consideration. These problems are best averted at the outset by the therapist taking careful consideration of what his needs are. There are usually other therapists with lower fees that a patient can consult if he is not comfortable with this therapist's fee, and a decision to investigate different therapists is in the best interests of both parties.

PLACE, SETTING, AND SPACE

Psychotherapy necessitates that the patient and the therapist agree to meet in some place. This is a simple and concrete aspect of the contract, so automatic it may seem unnecessary to discuss.

The patient likely expects to meet the therapist at a professional office, unless the patient is hospitalized. But the physical necessity of a place to meet does become a concern in certain instances of psychotherapy practice and, more important, the place is the concrete foundation for the metaphors that most interest the analytic therapist about the setting and space of the analytic relationship.

The concrete place of meeting is first important to the contract for psychotherapy in that the patient and therapist must agree to meet so that talking can begin. This simple issue seldom arises for the practicing psychotherapist in an established office. The patient and therapist readily agree to meet in the therapist's office, which is already arranged for the work of therapy. But the ease with which that occurs obscures the difficulties that some therapists have surmounted, perhaps in days when psychotherapy was not so commonly sought or in situations removed from private practice settings. Greenson (1967) talks of working in military settings and the demands placed on him to create some sense of safety when conditions were far from suitable. Sanville (1991) describes her early days as a social worker going into the field and dealing with all manner of intrusions, but nonetheless creating a safe enough psychological place for therapy.

The therapist does well to pay attention to the place where the patient is met. This is the first screen onto which the patient's projections are directed and certain aspects of one's office may stimulate undesirable beginnings. Langs (1989) in particular makes detailed suggestions about office arrangements. I have already mentioned the necessary attention to arrangements that afford a sense of privacy. The office is a place for the patient, and the therapist's personal effects, especially such things as family pictures, distract from the setting and stimulate the patient unnecessarily. These are not such important concerns for other professionals, but the analytic therapist is intent on understanding the patient's fantasies, and direct stimulation of those fantasies complicates the process unnecessarily.

Greenson (1967) and Sanville (1991) describe difficulties and problems of space, and their solutions. Even as they surmount

the difficulties they begin to wonder about the meanings associated with the therapeutic place. Sanville noted patients' feelings
and experience of the place at the time she made a move to a
private office. She elaborates some patients' particular attachment of meanings to aspects of her office. Stone (1961) speaks of
the setting of analysis and comments on the way it is taken for
granted, yet notes that the analytic setting is a rich and essential
aspect of the effectiveness of analytic therapy. The concern is first
for a place that affords adequate privacy so that an atmosphere of
safety may be provided. The therapist must be aware of this need
so that the place of meeting becomes part of the contract for
psychotherapy. Then the meanings and importance of place and
analytic space can be explored and developed in the analytic
dyad.

The most explicit use of the concept of space is initiated by
Winnicott (1971). He moves our understanding of the place in
which the therapy occurs to the richest metaphor of place or
setting. His foundation is the shared space of experience that
occurs between the mother and infant. This is a model for the
therapy relationship that has been developed further by writers
including Ogden (1989) and Sanville (1991), among many
others. The usefulness of this concept rests on the successful
creation of an environment where these experiences can be
explored. The physical environment is only a metaphor for the
more important psychological space necessary for therapy, as the
mother–infant dyad is a metaphor for the potential space that
Winnicott develops.

These concepts of space and place underscore the nature of
the contract for psychotherapy. A contract is an agreement about
a variety of realistic concerns for the person starting therapy,
including the therapist, fees, meeting place, schedule, and re-
sponsibilities. But in the analytic relationship the unconscious
meanings of the contract and the ways those meanings are
negotiated make up the work of the therapy. The negotiation of
this space and the experience that the patient has are what will
propel the development of the transference and the ultimate
understanding that analytic therapy intends to accomplish.

THE HIDDEN CONTRACT

Another consideration attaching to the contract for conducting therapy has to do with how private and how individual the treatment will be. Formal analysis and much of psychoanalytically oriented psychotherapy has assumed an individual adult patient capable of engaging a therapist independently of any other person. Therapists typically resist including relatives, friends, and seemingly concerned others in the consultation. Even the laws of confidentiality here protect both therapist and patient from the intrusions of others. But especially with the patient in crisis, therapy will begin in other ways and sometimes with other individuals present. Psychoanalytic therapy is begun with the intention to create a space where the therapist and patient can work together without intrusion, a space in which fantasy can develop free of certain reality intrusions. Clearly, not all therapy begins this way. The therapist starting with a new patient must recognize the potential for such intrusions and in some cases deal directly with these realities in order to establish a suitable working alliance that will not be undermined. Some examples include the patient who is propelled to therapy by some other—a spouse, a parent (even adult patients who are dependent on parents show up with mothers and others), or those coming to treatment with court orders and legal demands. If the therapist chooses to work with such patients some attention must be paid to the third party. Therapists have a variety of approaches to these problems that involve working toward a relationship with the patient that is private and individual rather than one influenced by those outside of the relationship. These issues are rightly dealt with in a negotiation of how the therapy will go forward. I prefer the patient who arrives independently for the first meeting. In my earlier days of building a practice I was willing to meet with all sorts of patient presentations, but one must recognize that these beginnings are not ideal. The formation of a therapeutic alliance in a suitable space for the analytic therapist may require some preliminary work that serves to establish an alliance of sorts with these outsiders in order to protect the patient's privacy. These concerns are negotiated with the patient. The therapist is asserting the conditions deemed necessary to carry on the therapy. The patient who brings family members and others to a first session is simply presenting his life as he experiences it, and the negotiation then must involve an adjustment as to how that presentation is going to be made in the way the therapist can best work. Some education and tolerance will be necessary from the therapist to direct this initial meeting toward an ongoing arrangement for treatment.

Third Parties

The problems raised by a third party in the room, whether in reality or in fantasy, are myriad. Let's consider a few. The man sent to therapy by his spouse appears compliant to the therapist and enters the first session ready to do what the therapist wishes. The therapist attempts several times to encourage the man to speak about the concerns he has but he repeatedly responds with little emotional tone. It becomes apparent to the therapist after a while that it was the spouse who wanted the man to be in therapy. Somehow this misalliance must be worked out. The third party in the room cannot be ignored or the therapy is just for appearances to please the man's spouse and will never touch the anxiety in the patient who has come to the office. Patients such as this need not become early failures, though the therapist who recognizes the problem, explores the individual patient's motivation, and agrees not to pursue such a therapy has not really admitted defeat, but has rightly sent away a person who had no intention or desire to be a patient. If such a therapy is to work out, the individual before you must somehow become a patient. I listen through the early presentation, which often takes the form of "My wife says I am distant," or "My wife says I don't talk with her enough," or "My wife says I don't listen," assuring myself that this man is not yet here about some anxiety he feels. I suggest after a while that it might be more helpful to hear what *he* feels, and the degree to which the individual will engage in this exploration may make it possible to refocus the therapy on his needs rather than his spouse's requested improvements. Often at this point it becomes clear to both of us that this man is not here for himself. What may also become clear, however, is that the man does feel a good deal of anxiety about losing his wife or—perhaps the other way around—he feels anxiety about his fantasies of terminating the marriage. The therapy may then begin to focus on what this man wants, what causes him pain in the relationship, and what concerns of his might be addressed. In such an instance I have chosen quite consciously to reject a contract with the spouse and to attempt some arrangement with the individual in front of me.

Court Orders

All manner of court orders propel some people to therapy. Again, an unspoken contract may be formed with whatever court has mandated the therapy. It goes like this. Mr. X. comes to treatment because the court has ordered counseling to address his violent actions toward his wife. He explains the circumstances and defends some of his actions, being careful to cite some responsibility in the event. He indicates that his lawyer will be calling and that in six months he will need a letter stating that he has met the court requirement. He makes some indication that he does want this marriage to work and that it has been hellish living with this woman in the current state of affairs.

Consider the unconscious motivation inevitable in such an arrangement. Even if this individual can intellectually acknowledge some need for therapy, he has to please a judge whom the therapist does not know. He has to get a letter, and in order to do that he must meet some demands of this therapist. The patient attempts to accommodate any demands of the therapist and may in many ways look like a "good patient." In fact that is his intent. The therapist in all sincerity attempts to address the nature of the conflicts in the marriage and the underlying causes of the patient's violence and gets some cooperation from the patient. However, in time the therapist begins to recognize a sense of futility, perhaps a sense that none of the expected negative reactions appear in any prominent way in the transference. Or perhaps at some point the patient finally erupts over some matter such as payment of the fee and the therapy is threatened with termination. The problem here is that both therapist and patient have entered into a collusion to meet the demands of the court and to that end no particularly useful connection or experience that might be analyzed can occur in the transference relationship. The patient is understandably anxious about the outcome of any negative reactions to the therapist and the therapist may even be happily engaged with this compliant patient. But the only goal being met is the court order. If the power and usefulness of analytic therapy are to take place some other program must be implemented. Many analytic therapists refuse such arrangements, although this situation is not so unlike that of the patient who seeks treatment in compliance with a spouse. Thus, these outside parties and the hidden contracts they imply must be acknowledged in the first session. To the extent that such contracts are not acknowledged and integrated into the therapy the above scenario is more likely to occur. I think that the therapist involved in such a hidden contract ultimately begins to feel a lack of interest in the work with the patient in the office as well as a discouraging loss of effectiveness.

Court orders, workers' compensation cases, and personal injury cases are more difficult to sort out than the case of the reluctant spouse. The problem here is that there is likely no way to break the contract with the court or the third-party payor. In fact, therapist arrangements with insurance companies and managed-care companies similarly set up a hidden contract. The therapist is listening to the patient with a split attention that overrides the contract with the patient. If this is not acknowledged then the therapist has entered into a duplicitous relationship with the patient; if it is acknowledged at the outset, the therapist has alerted the patient to the fact that she is listening with a split attention.

Regarding the intrusions of the court, I have tried several remedies with patients who present with these demands. When a person calls for therapy with the request for treatment under a workers' compensation lien, I indicate my willingness to work with the person, but that I do not accept liens. If the person wishes to engage in treatment and pay as she goes I will be happy to provide whatever diagnostic reports are necessary to obtain reimbursement. Often enough the therapy does not proceed any further. If it does proceed, it must still be acknowledged that a good report is necessary and that the patient is susceptible to some other motivation than getting better. In other cases of court orders I offer my services to treat, but I indicate that any evaluation for the court must come from an outside evaluator with whom I will share only the information that the patient has attended so many sessions. This is often acceptable to attorneys and closes the door both to part of the loss of confidentiality and to the patient's anxiety that some negative experience with me will jeopardize his evaluation for the court.

Parents and Other Parties

Parents of patients are a more difficult type of third party to deal with. I am particularly interested in the parents of adult patients, who are often in the position of paying for part or all of the treatment. Child therapists have long been dealing with the realistic issues necessitated by the parents' involvement in the child's therapy. But often enough we treat older adolescents and young adults who rely on parental support for their treatment. Some of the parents are willing to stay in the background, particularly those who have engaged in their own therapy and understand the value of their child's autonomous relationship with the therapist. Even when that is the case I try to make the contract as much as possible with the patient, explaining his responsibility to deal with parents around issues of payment of fees and so on. This may bring to light many important conflicts even at the outset and certainly serves to avert potential difficulties if the parent refuses to pay at some later date. If parents insist on being involved in some way the therapist must make additional efforts to deal with their concerns and educate them on the need for confidentiality and privacy. Again, if this is arranged well at the outset fewer problems arise later.

Even the recent changes in limits of confidentiality imply these hidden contracts. Mandated abuse reporting and duties to warn create a contract between the therapist and the legal system. While in many cases this may not be a strong factor, it is still presently inherent in our work with all patients today. Bollas and Sundelson (1995) have addressed this issue in detail, noting the growing list of intruders that the individual patient does not necessarily intend to bring to the first session. Laws that mandate the therapist to breach confidentiality, the intrusion of health-care payors, and the requirements for informed consent are all intruders into the work of analytic therapy. These demands are recent developments that affect the therapeutic space and the negotiation of that space. They place requirements on the thera-pist that many analytic therapists do not hold helpful in their therapeutic endeavors, but to which therapist and patient must make some adjustment.

THE FUNDAMENTAL RULE AND THE COUCH

Formal analysis typically utilizes several conditions not necessar-ily employed by the psychoanalytic psychotherapist. The expec-tation of a higher frequency of meetings, usually at least four times per week, has been discussed earlier. Freud (1913) empha-sized the fundamental rule: that the patient was expected to say all that came to her mind without any effort to edit. Much has been written about this technique and the varying success of its use. It is clear that all patients fail the expectation and that the analysis occurs around the nature of those failures. Analytically oriented psychotherapy nonetheless depends on the individual saying as much as possible of the fantasy and contents of his thinking. In contemporary psychoanalysis there is some variation as to whether the fundamental rule is stated explicitly or left implicit, and whether it is even worth stating given the immedi-ate emergence of resistances that must be dealt with in the analysis; stating the fundamental rule is thus seen as a kind of cognitive education that is not so valuable in the face of resis-tance and the pressure of the unconscious. However, whether used or not and whether in psychoanalysis proper or psycho-therapy, the fundamental rule is negotiated in the contract, usually in the early stages. The trained analyst would typically have a means of presenting this expectation that arises from training and personal style.

Use of the couch is more specifically in the domain of formal analysis. Surely the couch is used by some in psychotherapy, but more regularly its use is an expectation of the analyst. This is most clearly a moment of negotiation, because to the naive patient, lying on the couch may seem somewhat unusual, and the suggestion is often met with significant resistance. It is not my purpose here to discuss the value of using the couch or even the manner in which a therapist may encourage it. These are issues of formal analytic technique. Rather, I note the use of the couch since it may be a first-session issue that is primarily an expectation of the therapist and must be entered into the contract in some manner. If it is one of the therapist's conditions, the patient must have a means of understanding the request and analyzing her reactions. In practice, the use of the couch will likely be an item discussed at least several sessions later after some determination that analysis is the treatment of choice, and that it is part of the analyst's conditions of treatment.

CONSENT, DISCLOSURE, AND WRITTEN CONTRACTS

Paperwork has become a necessary part of the psychotherapist's work. It is an unwelcome task, but the sensible psychotherapist remains informed about what is required by the state licensing board of her profession and by the various ethical codes. The contemporary psychotherapist must find a means of meeting these demands. Caudill (1997), a California attorney who has defended many psychotherapists, states without ambivalence that the psychotherapist must have written notes, a written contract with the patient stating the fee and cancellation policy, a signed consent to treatment showing that the limits of confidentiality have been explained, and other written documentation about the beginning of a case. Each psychotherapist must become knowledgeable about the specific demands of her particular license, whether in psychology, marriage and family counseling, psychiatry, or social work. But the broadly stated demands are the same for all, as described by Caudill, who has met the problem after the lawsuit has been filed or the complaint taken up by a licensing board. Therapists practicing in an increasingly litigious society do well to protect themselves and remain realistic about the dangers.

Therapist's Notes

Paperwork does not arise out of the clinical needs of the patient or the therapist. Therapists have taken notes and mused on paper to themselves about the words, fantasies, and actions of their patients since the beginning of psychotherapy. Freud (1912b) even makes recommendations about how the analyst might take notes—at the end of the day, not in session, and not to the distraction of the patient or the therapist's attention. Psychotherapists have debated the pros and cons of when and whether to take notes as well as who might see the notes, and the privacy of those notes. Some therapists have always taken notes and some have only taken notes for certain purposes, but those notes were all for the therapist's use in the patient's best interest. Today, every therapist must take notes and retain paperwork; the patient's activities in the psychotherapy session must be documented. These are not notes for the patient's needs in treatment or to aid the therapist's thinking about a case; these are notes intended to protect the therapist in the event that the integrity of the therapy relationship is breached. Caudill (1997) titles his chapter on notes "Documentation: The Therapist's Shield."

This contemporary demand on the therapist stands in stark contradiction to one of the hallmarks of psychoanalytic psychotherapy: the promise of confidentiality. In the days when therapists took notes to help their thinking about a case, those notes were carefully protected. No other person knew of them, except perhaps a consulting therapist who treated the confidentiality of that patient with the same respect as the patient's therapist. But as therapists create documents of informed consent, intake information sheets, and notes defending their actions with a patient, it is inherent in the process that this information is written for a reader external to the privacy of that psychotherapy relationship.

Bollas and Sundelson (1995) present a forceful argument that analytic therapists begin to regain the privilege of confidentiality for psychotherapy, one that has been rapidly and extensively eroded in recent times. They describe the reasons why and the manner in which that privilege has been degraded and they wonder about the effect of such a wholesale loss of confidentiality. Many of the issues of this loss of confidentiality and the concomitant enlisting of therapists to monitor misbehavior in society come into play in the first session. The therapist starting with a new patient must understand the effects these influences have on the patient and on the beginning of the therapy.

Questions of Legal Exposure

The most immediate effect of these current demands is that therapists everywhere are now focused on the paperwork, the ever-increasing ethics codes, and the potential legal exposure they face each day. As has happened in other professions and industries that face this increase in legal liability, some therapists now shun more difficult patients in favor of those who present less exposure. Even as psychoanalysis has broadened the scope of who is deemed treatable, psychotherapists are hesitating to take on the very cases that might now be helped by the treatment. Therapists are less ready to meet the potential patient and less ready to hear the beginnings of transference when their attention is focused on the structure that must be set in place to effect legal protection. It used to be that establishing an adequate frame for treatment was an integral and important part of the patient's development of self boundaries. It has now become an activity focused on external demands and is affected by the possibility of a lawsuit against the therapist. This has eroded the therapist's concentration on the patient's needs.

Bollas and Sundelson (1995) also speak to an even more disturbing aspect of this change in legal requirements for the therapist. Therapists have become informants; their allegiance to the patient is betrayed by their mandated responsibility to the state. A simple stated or written disclosure of the limits of confidentiality cannot adequately address the unconscious effects of this new role for therapists. The patient no longer enjoys an atmosphere of safety in the presence of a therapist who is bound and committed to protecting the privacy of the relationship. The therapist has another allegiance, another role, that takes attention away from the patient, skews the therapist's authority with respect to the patient, and damages the safety necessary for psychotherapy to proceed.

The patient has also become a source of danger for the therapist. Hedges and colleagues (1999) note that they have heard many times from therapists who have lost their licenses, who had felt it could not happen to them. They encourage a more realistic view of the current state of affairs—yet the very thought that it could happen sets up an unconscious expectation of danger for the therapist. Every patient that a therapist meets with for a first session is a potential liability.

Note-taking

Each instance of paperwork deserves attention in the spirit of an analytic first session as it affects or threatens the therapy relationship. Items Caudill (1997) lists as essential include progress notes (including intake, ongoing, and termination notes), consent to treatment, and a signed contract. Note-taking as an aid to treatment is a matter of personal preference. Notes have been used by therapists to assist in presentations for consultation and for purposes of research and writing. The question of whether to take notes in session is a highly individual matter. Some therapists find note-taking an aid to attention while others find it a distraction. Freud found it distracting. Patients also have an influence on this, as some find the note-taking, even when it is done out of their field of vision as they lie on the couch, full of meaning and concern. Some patients will make a huge conflict of the note-taking as it is analyzed and negotiated with the therapist. Others are disappointed to find the therapist does not wish to note their every word. Each therapist will find a particular preference, and in fact it may make sense for each therapeutic dyad to work out a suitable method. These are matters that have always been a source of query in the psychotherapy relationship as the therapist sets about working in the transference.

The demand for notes from a third party is another matter. State licensing boards require notes that might at some point be viewed by someone other than the therapist, the patient, or the therapist's consultant. Defending attorneys are suggesting the careful documentation of psychotherapy so that these notes can be entered into a public forum if the therapist is sued. And notes document the various mandated reports a therapist might have to make about a patient. These requirements for notes implicitly breach the confidentiality of the psychotherapy relationship. This affects the atmosphere of safety, the attention of the therapist, and changes how the therapist's own notes, previously a personal record, are taken. Consider one of Caudill's (1997) recommendations: that any sexual reference made by a patient be noted. In the past, a patient's references to sexual thoughts and feelings surely drew the attention of the therapist. The analytic therapist, of course, would wonder about an emerging erotic transference and might even muse about the pleasures and difficulties such a transference presents. The therapist might then encourage further exploration of these feelings as the patient is ready, recognizing the feelings of shame and embarrassment that often arise in patients as such material emerges. These are all well-accepted actions of the therapist. But the atmosphere of reporting and shielding oneself has dramatically affected the process a therapist will use with such a presentation currently. Perhaps today as the patient makes some sexual reference the therapist will first think about whether the patient is about to refer to child abuse. The therapist might check the time to calculate the statutory limits for making a report, and wonder whether she has the proper forms in the files. Or the therapist might try to remember what exactly Caudill (1997) said about noting these references and how a judge or attorney might read the notes. The therapist will be inclined to think back to any other contacts with the patient that might have been misconstrued and whether there were references that went unnoticed, or whether the therapist acted in some countertransferential manner that encouraged the patient. Then the caring therapist will also feel protective toward the patient and worry about how to note these references so as not to hurt the patient who is sincere and not likely to sue. After all of this, is there time to focus on the work of analyzing the transference or has it been so muddled with outside concerns and anxiety as to be lost in this session? The current demands on the therapist constitute hidden contracts with outside agencies, future defense attorneys, and others not part of the patient's treatment. Such trends greatly affect the way psychotherapy is conducted today.

Despite all of this, the effect of note-taking may be minimized by the therapist. Notes can be taken outside the patient's awareness, and in the greatest percentage of cases notes can be protected. Therapists are finding ways of dealing with documentation requirements that only need limited attention and allow them to remain focused on the patient. Much of what is detrimental in the actual act of taking notes can be kept within the therapist's private work. This is not so with other paperwork requirements.

Written Contracts

The consent for treatment and any signed contract must be handled directly with the patient. These are demands that underscore the damage that has already occurred to the patient's privilege of confidentiality. As paperwork, these documents are not so disturbing to patients, as they are likely to be familiar with similar paperwork other health care professionals require. Other health care professionals, however, are not concerned or readily affected by the meanings a patient applies to the paperwork. The psychotherapist is, and recognizes that consent forms contain many potential stimuli to unwanted meanings. A consent form must contain statements about the dangers and potential experiences a person might expect in psychotherapy, the fact that other treatments may serve similar functions or provide better results, and that confidentiality is limited in cases of child abuse, threats of violence, elder abuse, and when the patient enters mental health into a court proceeding. In addition, confidentiality is immediately limited by the use of certain types of insurance, especially managed care, which requires forms and reports from the therapist.

The potential meanings that a new patient might apply to such statements are myriad and threatening to the therapy. Consider the possible effects on the paranoid patient, or the borderline patient (i.e., one who has seldom experienced safe boundaries), let alone the direct effect on the person seeking help for impulses to violence or molestation. Hedges (1999) states that pedophiles have long since stopped seeking treatment because they know that it will only lead to reporting. These mandates have had the effect of keeping out of treatment people most in need of it.

A written contract is now considered necessary for beginning with a new patient. The written contract must include a statement of the agreed-upon fee and a statement of the cancellation policy. This is the minimal information suggested by Caudill (1997). He makes some further suggestions from a legal perspective that the therapist may wish to include after getting advice from an attorney. Again, Caudill is looking at this from the retrospective point of view of having to defend a therapist who is already in some legal contest. Presumably, Caudill's recommendations arise from instances in which the therapist's statement of the fee and cancellation policy have been unclear, and in some later conflict the patient has felt injured or coerced by demands that were not settled.

Clearly there is a wide range of potential real and transference conflicts in these matters. In the history of psychotherapy therapists and patients have struggled with these very boundaries. Looked at even more broadly, these matters make for conflicts in all areas of human commerce. For psychotherapy today we have the added danger of a patient taking the conflict into court or to a licensing board, so the recommendations serve to alert us to areas of danger. These changes in society take the therapist's attention away from the work of the psychotherapy, the traditional arena for struggling with these realities of time and money that are rich with transference meaning.

A contract is necessary for psychotherapy. As discussed at

length earlier, a contract is an implicit, if not explicit, part of any human relationship. A contract must be agreed on for psychotherapy to begin, even if it is poorly conceived or if both parties fail to acknowledge aspects of it. However the contract may be decided between the two participants in a psychotherapy relationship, a formal written document does not make it any more significant. In fact the pressure for codification of our contract with patients has done more to trivialize the contract and our work than to elevate its importance. The written contract that now can be offered as part of a practice package by some publisher is no longer the very personal agreement between patient and therapist that was traditionally the foundation of the beginnings of psychotherapy. The written contract may seem to serve the purpose of correcting the practice of unskilled, unfair, or even malicious therapists, but it also replaces an important aspect of the initiation of psychotherapy by circumventing the spoken, negotiated agreement for treatment that in the past is how two individuals started this process.

The broader issues these laws and mandates raise require action from our professional organizations. Bollas and Sundelson (1995) have outlined a plan of action for psychoanalysts and psychoanalytic therapists that aims at regaining the privilege of confidentiality for psychotherapy. These are not changes that will be won by one psychotherapist, though some individual therapists have suffered major court expenses and loss of practice in trying to resist the changes in confidentiality.

Ethical Responsibilities

For the therapist facing first sessions in this climate some important considerations must be part of the treatment agreement. First, these impingements on the psychotherapy relationship cannot be ignored. The therapist who fails to document or obtain consent, who does not delineate the limits of confidentiality, or establish fee and cancellation policies with the patient risks difficulties with licensing boards and the courts. But, more important, the therapist who tries to avoid these issues by denial only fails to recognize that patients know about these matters, or can find out. It is not an analytic stance to let matters known to the therapist come into the patient's awareness through another source. This creates an atmosphere of unsafety. Each therapist must find ways to present these matters to the new patient with honesty. One must not deny the policies and ethics that direct this field; the patient at least unconsciously knows that each therapist must be aligned with these policies or an attitude of dishonesty enters into the treatment at the outset. However, a therapist may choose to work in a manner inconsistent with these policies owing to ethical or philosophical rejection of them. Bollas and Sundelson (1995) cite some therapists who have taken this path. This is a decision that has inherent risks, and the basis for making such a choice and the means of working with patients in congruence with that position are not in the scope of this book.

Until analytic therapists are able to change these policies and educate agencies and the courts as to why privilege is so important to this work, therapists will have to find ways of working with patients around the presently necessary paperwork. How the therapist presents this material is the most important aspect of handling these matters in an analytic way; they must be entered into the therapeutic relationship as part of the negotiations and communications in beginning treatment. Matters of disclosure and limits of confidentiality must be discussed in the early stages of therapy, not because boards mandate this, but because the therapist would otherwise be leaving some matters outside of the session and relationship, an action that is antithetical to an analytic stance. Freud (1913) warned of the patient who attempted to place some matters outside of the analytic relationship. His warning rightly refers to therapists' actions as well.

Presenting a consent-to-treatment form and a contract can wait until near the end of the first session, a time when matters of fee and schedule are typically handled. More time will be necessary than used to be taken to simply establish a fee and next appointment. Trying to handle these matters at the beginning of the session will give a message to the patient that the therapist's concerns about money and schedule take precedence over what is on the patient's mind, especially as the paperwork discussed here is largely the therapist's concern, since it is necessary to protect the therapist from legal liabilities.

To begin to discuss matters of fee and schedule marks a significant point. In many first sessions most of the time is taken up with the patient's concerns and the patient's description of his life. It is when business matters are discussed that the therapist's needs and expectations come fully into the psychotherapy. Only the most disturbed patient expects the therapist to provide the therapy without a fee or to be always available, so most patients are prepared consciously for the discussion of business matters and even for the paperwork discussed above. The analytic therapist must be prepared for the unconscious reactions and meanings created at this point.

The increased amount of paperwork in therapy practice must not lead the therapist to overlook the necessity of going over all aspects of this material with the patient. Typical business practice and legal recommendations insist that the contract and forms must be reviewed. But for the therapist, the more important issue is that the patient must be aware of all aspects of the therapy, not for legal reasons but for reasons of transference meanings. The therapist must know if the patient has a paranoid reaction to the reporting of disclosures, or if there is any indication that these limits of confidentiality will create areas of resistance or anxiety that will hinder the therapy or threaten a therapeutic alliance.

It is an offensive practice for a therapist to use paperwork as a shield from the anxieties of discussing difficult issues. For example, some therapists have used a contract to detail stringent cancellation policies that they fear to discuss openly with the patient. Thus a new patient may be handed a packet of materials, take them home, sign the forms, but may not read them or may forget the policy before it ever comes into play. If the therapist is going to stand by a policy, he must be able and willing to discuss this policy directly with the patient. It is dishonest to create a contract in which one party is unaware of the details and remedies in the contract and it is poor clinical technique to surprise the patient with something that the therapist is too anxious to negotiate directly. When Caudill (1997) suggests a contract that details the fee and cancellation policy, it appears that he is writing to therapists who have insisted on payment of a fee for a canceled session without any attention to clear discussion of the policy or empathy for whatever misunderstanding or transference use of the policy the patient has made. Surely any therapist can give up one session's fee in order to adequately negotiate a policy with the patient at the moment the problem arises.

As this paperwork has become necessary to psychotherapy practice, it requires of the therapist that each aspect of the contract, the consent form, and the various disclosures be reviewed with the new patient, and that the various forms be given to the patient for careful reading. Hedges (1999) indicates that he now uses a multipage form when contracting for ongoing therapy or analysis. But, he makes the form into a process of communication between the patient and himself. He requests that the patient write all over the form, asking questions, noting places where it might be adjusted to this relationship, and so on. He has thus managed to take an onerous task demanded by a litigious society and make it part of the psychotherapy and the process of discovery.

Sample Forms

I have devised several forms for use in my practice. The forms are readily changed when necessary and in most cases I make a form on the word processor for each new patient. The first form is an example of my intake notes. I have tried to make it simple, requiring little writing, so that I can complete the form soon after seeing the patient and just file it, which leads to minimal distraction of my attention. The patient does not see this form. It is simply used to create a beginning file. In addition to this I file a mental-status form. This form meets the requirements of documentation. My attention to a new patient seeking analytic therapy is not especially served by this form, but the information it contains is accurate and allows me to reduce my attention to paperwork to a minimum.

PETER S. ARMSTRONG, Ph.D.   **INTAKE FORM**

License Number: XXXX

Name: _____

Address: _____

Phone: _____ DOB: _____ SSN: _____

Referral: _____

Presenting complaint:

History:

Family history of: ☐ mental illness   ☐ suicide   ☐ substance abuse

    Comment:

Previous treatment   ☐ outpatient   ☐ inpatient   ☐ none

    Comment:

Records request   ☐ requested   ☐ patient declined   ☐ not requested

☐ Reviewed with patient possible referrals for medication, other therapies, etc.

Referrals made:

    ☐ None

Fees: A fee of $ _____ was agreed to by the patient, to be paid each session.

Plan: Patient agreed to _____ sessions per week psychotherapy (90806) to address concerns of presenting complaint.

Comments:

☐ Patient was informed: (1) that all matters of treatment were negotiable and fully within his or her control to accept or reject; (2) that other therapies may provide similar or better results; (3) that the therapist makes no claim about the superiority of this therapy over other available treatments.

☐ Confidentiality: The limits of confidentiality were explained to the patient and the patient was invited to question any aspect of the contract for psychotherapy.

The following form serves as a signed consent and contract. Near the end of the session I go over business matters with the patient, as described in other sections of this book. By the time I give this letter to the patient I have already discussed all of the details of the consent. If necessary I can change this form before the patient signs it by reprinting a letter specific to the negotiations a particular patient and I have made. I often include some additional information for the naive patient, which describes psychotherapy and discusses the use of insurance benefits. Most of all I encourage the further and extended discussion of all of this material. This is so that possible misunderstanding is dealt with early in treatment and so I am able to observe this patient in the midst of all of our interactions.

PETER S. ARMSTRONG, Ph.D.

Psychoanalysis and Psychotherapy [phone number]

Now that we have met for the first session of psychotherapy I want you to have some information about how I conduct psychotherapy and some details about the business arrangements for treatment. I have enclosed several brochures. Please feel free to question any of this information and discuss it with me in session. I will explain any of the statements below in more detail or anything that is unclear.

NATURE OF THE TREATMENT

Psychotherapy can be a profound life-changing experience. I believe that people can change at any stage of life, but that some hard work may go into those changes. As you already know, this is a process that is quite different from going to your medical doctor. All business is conducted directly with me; I answer my own phone calls, negotiate the fee, and schedule my own appointments. This will help us learn to deal with each other in the process of psychotherapy, it keeps overhead expenses down, and does not involve any other person in your treatment. Everything about the work of psychotherapy is worthy of discussion and I encourage you to bring up your questions or concerns directly with me in the session. Psychotherapy is a professional service, but the contact you have with me is very personal; therefore I hope that we can deal with all matters of your treatment in a direct way, talking to each other.

CONFIDENTIALITY AND INTRUSIONS

Psychotherapy is a very private treatment. I feel strongly that all of the concerns you talk about with me should be kept completely confidential. There are some times when I cannot ensure your confidentiality. If you use insurance in any form the insurer will request a diagnosis at the very least. Increasingly, insurers are requiring more extensive information. I will not send information or talk with an insurer without your knowledge and I will not send reports without your approval.

I will not talk to any family member, friend, employer, or other interested party about your treatment unless you and I have discussed this in detail in session. I will not even return their phone calls until you and I have spoken. There are four instances, legally mandated, in which I cannot ensure confidentiality. They are: when a patient introduces his or her mental condition into civil litigation; when a threat of violence is made against a third party; instances of child abuse; and instances of elder abuse. If any of these statements are unclear please talk directly with me about them.

PAYMENT OF FEES AND USE OF INSURANCE

I ask that you pay my fee directly to me at the beginning of each session. You are responsible for payment regardless of whether you choose to use insurance coverage. Insurance coverage has advantages and disadvantages. Typically, I am not covered by any managed-care plan, health management organization, or preferred provider plan. I may be covered by traditional indemnity insurance or covered as a nonparticipating provider in other plans. You must talk with your insurer to determine whether or not my services are covered. At your request I will provide a statement with all necessary billing and payment information that you can submit to your insurance carrier. It is important to determine just how much coverage you have and whether the loss of confidentiality is worth the benefit. I have chosen to remain independent of these insurance plans because they intrude on your privacy in psychotherapy and limit your choices in treatment decisions. I encourage you to discuss any questions about this with me.

CANCELLATION OF APPOINTMENTS

I expect you to be responsible for the fee for any session that you miss without notifying me in advance. If you must cancel an appointment, I expect you to provide adequate notice or to be responsible for the session fee. If you expect some unusual or special circumstances regarding cancellation of appointments please discuss this with me so that we can negotiate a means of dealing with this between us as the necessity arises.

CONTACTING ME

Contact me through my office voice mail at [phone number]. I check these messages regularly throughout the day from early morning to late evening and on weekends. If I do not return your call in a timely manner please leave another message; as you know, electronic messaging sometimes fails. If I am unable to return your call, due to vacation or travel, I will indicate that in my message and I may have another professional available to return urgent calls. If you have some sort of emergency I expect that you will contact the appropriate emergency agency, your physician, or a hospital emergency room. In most cases I believe that any concern you have can be best dealt with in a session.

TERMINATION OF TREATMENT

Most likely the decision to end psychotherapy will occur naturally as you accomplish your goals and establish a process of personal growth. I hope, as our work together proceeds and your sense of relationship with me deepens, that the decision to terminate will be one that you discuss with me frankly, and that we can use that decision to further your self understanding. The decision to enter psychotherapy is your choice. The decision to end psychotherapy must also be your choice. While I hope that it will be a decision that we can consider together you may of course end your contract with me at any time.

Consent to Treatment.

I _____ have read the above information and discussed my questions with Dr. Armstrong. I consent to psychotherapy treatment with Dr. Armstrong as described above.

_____   _____   _____

Print Name   Signature   Date

_____

Peter S. Armstrong, Ph.D.

CLOSING WORDS ON CONTRACT

The contract for psychotherapy is an agreement between two individuals to meet and work together in a unique personal and professional relationship. It is as inherent to the working together as the implicit or explicit contract of any human relationship. Whether or not the therapist pays attention to the development of the contract, one exists. It is necessary in the first session to acknowledge this agreement and to make clear the expectations of each party in order to avoid problems later in the treatment. The contract for psychotherapy contains the frame or boundaries of the therapy; it protects both patient and therapist and acknowledges that each has limits as to what can be done within this relationship. These limits are not simply rules taught to students of therapy but boundaries that are necessary to conduct psychotherapy. These are guidelines that have grown from the successful and the failed experiences of many prior psychotherapists.

The contract for psychotherapy acknowledges that each participant of the therapeutic dyad has limits, expectations, and needs in the relationship, analogous to those in any human relationship. It contains the ethic of the work of psychotherapy that these limits exist and that the therapist does not exploit the patient. Similarly the patient must not exploit the therapist, but this impulse in the patient must be contained by the therapist and is a subject of the analysis. In contemporary practice many aspects of the contract for psychotherapy have been concretized in policies and legal demands for the therapist to act in some particular manner with the patient. While many of these demands contain a germ of accuracy regarding a professional relationship that does not exploit, the codification of the psychotherapy contract has diminished the therapist's freedom of judgment and constrained the development of a contract that reflects the specific needs of a unique therapeutic dyad. Along with this, a cornerstone of psychotherapy, the promise of confidentiality, has been severely eroded. It is a challenge for the contemporary therapist to maintain a safe enough atmosphere for the patient and meet the increasing requirements of our field.

Chapter 5

Assessment

I've heard Gregg's voice on the phone, we've agreed to meet for a first session, and now I've observed him as he entered my office and began talking in response to my minimal introduction of the therapy session. I track Gregg's way of presenting himself and in concert with this I track my own private associations and fantasies as he speaks. I notice certain anxieties he has stirred in me, some concerns about similar men who have challenged my ways of practice out of their own anxieties about beginning. I wonder what will make this feel like a safe enough environment for Gregg and what concerns have motivated his consultation. I'm struck at first by how so many things Gregg tells me seem to be going okay for him, how little he complains of aspects of his life. I imagine that his entrance into my office has raised his defenses against whatever pain caused him to call me. I think to myself that I'll have to help him find that pain again in a way that will propel him to use the therapy and use me, but not discourage him. At the moment of our first contact and throughout the first session I begin to consider what this man is presenting and what it might mean.

ASSESSMENT—THE THERAPIST'S CRAFT

Assessment is the foundation of the psychotherapist's craft. The therapist begins assessment on first hearing a potential patient's voice on the telephone and only ends as the patient says goodbye at the close of the last session. Each intervention begins and ends with assessment and the therapist is assessing the advancement of transference and countertransference even when the patient is absent. Assessment is a vast topic, an activity in which the whole profession of mental health is involved. Treatment decisions hinge on psychological and psychiatric assessments, as do job selections and forensic determinations. Methods of assessment range from the day-to-day use of countertransference by the psychotherapist to the highly structured, research-designed assessments of objective and projective testing. In the field of mental health, assessment has as much to do with activities unrelated to psychotherapy as those related to it.

In this exploration it is necessary to narrow the topic to the practice of analytic psychotherapy and to determine the scope of assessment for the first session. I will discuss the common methods and approaches to assessment with a view to isolating the activities and techniques that are most useful in analytic therapy and most important to the first session of psychotherapy. In general terms, the primary goal of assessment for psychotherapy at the very beginning of treatment is to determine if the patient is appropriate for the treatment and if the practicalities and realities the treatment demands can be adjusted to this particular patient and psychotherapist. If these issues cannot be satisfactorily addressed in the first or several beginning sessions, treatment will not proceed or it will end in a disappointment for both patient and therapist. Later, the purpose of assessment shifts to the identification of specific problems and the understanding of how the patient responds to interventions.

In order to set the stage for observation and understanding of the transference, initial assessment activities must be consistent with the process of creating the atmosphere for a therapeutic alliance between therapist and patient. This is a key thesis of this book: *the patient's experience of the therapist and expression of transference is a spontaneous development in the therapy from the outset and must be observed from the very beginning.* The therapist's approach to assessment must take this into account. A variety of assessment techniques are worthy of discussion as the starting point for psychotherapy. But in general the first session and initial assessment must show the way that all later assessment will take place. In the middle phases of psychotherapy, when a therapeutic alliance has been effected and the work is thoroughly in progress, the detailed work of assessment goes on day by day. The psychotherapist is forming hypotheses from observations, from the patient's reported feelings and fantasies, from the unconscious projections and identifications experienced in the transference, and from enactments by the patient. Assessment precedes each interpretation and then follows the patient's response to the interpretation. This is an ongoing process throughout the therapy, one set in motion at the first session.

In the beginning of treatment the therapist relies on this same material, but it is not developed or experienced in depth. The patient is new to the therapist and initial anxieties may even cloud early assessments until more familiarity is gained with this patient. Because the safety and stability of a therapeutic alliance have yet to be formed adequately, the therapist needs to be more cautious about speculations and interventions. The patient's pain, anxiety, and motivation for treatment are unknown, and the ways in which empathy can be communicated by the therapist are as yet untested.

Later assessments in psychotherapy are part of an ongoing work that rests on a therapeutic alliance. Early assessments in psychotherapy are often impelled by a need to reach a conclusion or decision. Later assessments are not so determined by those needs. Assessments for purposes other than psychotherapy often call for assessment decisions. The forensic examiner and the inpatient intake evaluator must provide conclusions that direct decisions within a certain limited time frame. The psychotherapist beginning a long-term therapy does not have to make such determinations so rapidly. Long-term psychotherapy actually may be distinguished from other therapies, especially the short-term and active therapies, by the reduced demand for assessment decisions in the later stages of psychotherapy. The therapist beginning a long-term treatment is trying to create an atmosphere in which the pressure for decisions is lessened and assessment decisions are minimized in frequency, one in which a comfortable amount of time can be spent on careful observation and exploration.

In contemporary practice, increasing demands have been placed on the therapist to make assessment decisions at many points within the therapy. The focus of early assessments has been mandated to be upon suicidality, child abuse, other forms of abuse, medication needs, and the therapist's level of competence. These are demands made by laws and policies affecting our profession. They are demands that call for action, rather than analysis, even when the data are unclear or unexplored. More important, these are demands that take the focus of attention away from the patient's needs and away from the balanced, careful observation by a therapist that will slow down the need for action and begin to create an analytic atmosphere in which the depths of the person's conflicts can be explored without intrusion. Some of these assessment decisions called for by contemporary law and policy are for the apparent good of society more than the patient. In the worst instances, where an insurer or other third party is watching over the treatment, assessment decisions are for cost savings and employers' needs rather than the patient's needs. These decisions take attention away from the patient's experience and the reasons for that experience.

In contrast to earlier days of outpatient psychotherapy, a wider range of patients now seek psychotherapy or are coerced to seek therapy. The courts regularly require psychotherapy for offenders of different types and for individuals involved in marital and custody disputes. As these patients seek psychotherapy the potential that a new patient might be dangerous has increased. Obviously in such instances the ethical therapist will make assessment decisions and act to protect herself, the patient, or others. Many of these decisions, as currently mandated, must be made within specified time limits, whether or not corroborating information is available. These demands on the therapist necessarily intrude on all patients' confidentiality and undermine the professional judgment of the therapist. Even though these laws are also designed to protect the therapist for breaching confidentiality, they have the effect of undermining confidentiality in all psychotherapy.

There are two reasons for the proliferation of such mandates. One is that the range of therapists now licensed to practice has been enlarged, while the extent of training needed to reach licensure ranges from rather minimal to the rigors of doctoral level work. There are many ways to obtain a license and the public does not easily distinguish one from the other. The laws are aimed at the lowest common denominator and thereby limit the professional judgment of those who are highly trained. A second reason for the increase of mandates on the psychotherapist is captured very eloquently in the book *The Death of Common Sense* (Howard 1994). The writer, a founding partner of a New York law firm, traces the philosophy behind the proliferation of laws—too many laws—that have replaced personal responsibility. The hope behind this is that enough proper laws will allow the country to run without human intervention. Of course that is not possible; but meanwhile we have undermined one of the very characteristics that psychotherapy seeks to develop in the individual: personal responsibility.

Another problem for the analytic therapist faced with mandates to report on such issues is that the way in which the therapist listens to a patient and sets the stage for an analytic process and collaboration in a sense handicaps the therapist as an assessor for reality issues. The analytic therapist is listening for the unconscious processes of the patient, the fantasies and object relationships that are represented in the conscious presentation and reported stories about the patient's life. This is a very different sort of assessment than the forensic assessor makes of the potentially dangerous criminal. Outsiders as well as patients ask for information or confirmations that the therapist cannot give; neither the manner through which the therapist obtains information nor the nature of that information provides the kind of evidence requested. Outsiders ask if this patient was actually abused by her father, if the patient is lying about her symptoms, or if she is ready to return to work. Patients ask for assurance that the remembered molestation is true, that the therapist believes their story. The therapist is being asked to speak as a witness to events that she has not witnessed, or to confirm the realistic validity of a patient's thoughts, fantasies, and memories, all of which psychoanalytic theory has long recognized as distorted by many factors in every person's experience.

The therapist cannot answer many of those questions with any confidence since there is no outside corroboration. To remain focused on the patient and the patient's unconscious is an activity antithetical to assessing these outside realities. The therapist is interested in the patient's experience, not in the evidence that a private investigator might seek. Perhaps a patient will feel some need to verify certain past experiences as a result of work in therapy, but the therapist cannot provide that verification from the way the patient has told the story. The work of psychotherapy may make the person a more honest reporter of experience, but the assessment of the veracity of the patient's reporting of history is not within the scope of the psychotherapist's available data.

Along with the proliferation of therapists, the term *psychotherapy* has become diluted. It no longer refers to a treatment aimed at suffering patients who independently seek treatment. Given this confusion some distinctions must be made. *Analytic psychotherapy* refers to a long-term relationship intent on making conscious a person's psychodynamics. Many other psychotherapies exist today and as a term psychotherapy is employed in other ways. Short-term therapies focus on crisis or specific symptom treatment. These approaches require a different first-session agenda. Therapies that aim to support a person in the face of acute crisis, and therapies that do not rest on a psychodynamic theory of development also approach the first session differently and make assessments from other theoretical frameworks.

The term *psychotherapy* is also applied to coerced therapies, such as those recommended for criminals or substance abusers, as when a court orders a course of psychotherapy. This also occurs in custody disputes and family violence. Many of the freedoms the patient enjoys in traditional psychotherapy are not available

here and the patient's choice and confidentiality are severely
restricted. These are valuable uses of mental health treatments to
be sure, but their limits must be understood. They are not the
powerful treatment of psychotherapy that is rooted in psychoanalysis. In analytic therapies, confidentiality is essential to
protect the development of the transference without the con-
founding influence of the therapist's real power affecting the
patient's future choices and freedoms.

Assessing for Treatment

As a broad principle for the first session, assessment decisions
must be kept to a minimum. The appropriate place for assessment decisions is in the hands of a forensic examiner or others
who must draw conclusions to answer some specific set of
questions within a very limited time frame. The analytic psychotherapist does not have to do this. The vital assessment performed by the analytic therapist is the assessment that takes place
over the entire course of the treatment. It is an assessment that
ends in the patient's self knowledge and his ability to carry on the
work without the therapist's presence. Rothstein (1990) elaborates the therapist's countertransference experience as one of the
most valuable assessment tools available to the analytic therapist.
But the use of countertransference is focused on observation and
understanding the patient, not on the formulation of assessment
decisions. This process requires a setting as free as possible of the
intrusion of demands for therapist action.

Of course some assessment decisions must be made in the first
session, although early assessments are often the most general.
The simplest and first decision is whether the person is requesting help with something that psychotherapy can address. Several
clear examples arose in my early practice. After I had set an
appointment with a young male caller, ostensibly requesting
psychotherapy, the man closed the phone call by explaining that,
of course, the judge would need a letter from me after the first
session. It soon became clear that all this man wanted was a
letter, after one or two sessions of "therapy," telling the judge
that he would never expose himself in public again. An assess-

ment decision is required in cases like this, especially since such men often have difficulty paying for services. The man could well use psychotherapy, but his request was for something quite distinct from psychotherapy. A therapist might, of course, make some kind of arrangement with this man for evaluation or whatever, but a simple, unassessed decision to proceed with therapy would likely meet a dead end.

An important, but often overlooked, early assessment decision is whether the therapist wishes to work with this patient. The patient may present some particularly difficult concern that the therapist, in an honest self-assessment, recognizes she is not willing to treat. A colleague of mine was referred a male perpetrator of child sexual abuse. Whether or not this man was actually motivated for treatment did not matter by the end of the first session. My colleague found the presenting problem too repulsive to feel she could be competent and empathic with this patient. Her assessment decision had nothing to do with the treatability of the man or his disorder, it had to do with her honest self-evaluation. It was a decision about the prognosis of this therapeutic dyad, and she judged it to be unlikely to succeed. Such an assessment decision would likely not be made very far into treatment, but it is essential at the beginning, although many decisions may not be as dramatic as this one. A therapist may decide not to take a patient for all manner of reasons, even that scheduling is not convenient. This is part of the therapist's responsibility to accurately assess her willingness to engage in a potentially lengthy relationship. A thorough assessment must include an assessment of the therapist, as part of the four-way assessment described below.

Therapists in the early stages of trying to build a private practice do well to be less selective about whom they choose to treat. The ability to choose one's patients is a luxury for the person satisfactorily in a full practice, or sufficiently supported by other income. Of course a therapist must assess his competence to treat any particular patient, but novice therapists must not be too selective about fees, schedules, or other matters if they hope to get a broad experience and to interest referral sources in using their services. In a clinic setting, where some preassessment has taken place and there is a regular flow of patients, the therapist may wish to be more selective, though it is useful in the early stages of learning to conduct psychotherapy to get a sense of the widest range of patients possible.

The setting in which the therapist works also has an influence on the assessment of the patient. Kernberg (1984) has written extensively about the assessment and treatment of borderline and narcissistic psychopathology. He devised, tested, and taught the use of an interview aimed at diagnosing these disorders. The setting in which it is used is an aspect of its methodology. Much of this work appears to be in a hospital setting, with patients likely to exhibit severe symptoms. Kernberg devised the technique in part for psychiatric residents in training, and thus it is a training technique for highly skilled individuals who had not had a great deal of psychotherapy experience. The interview provided a psychoanalytically oriented approach to learning about personality development and assessing patients for a variety of treatment options. Kernberg's approach is especially suited to a psychiatric hospital setting to which he brings a thoroughgoing psychoanalytic perspective.

Rothstein (1990) speaks to issues of assessment in private practice. He writes to psychoanalysts, but his conception may be applied by the analytic psychotherapist who does not conduct formal analysis. Rothstein is strongly committed to psychoanalysis. He works in private practice as an analyst and it is most likely that many individuals referred to him are already screened in some way. He asserts that psychoanalysis is the treatment of choice for most individuals who enter his office or for that matter the offices of other analysts. He is less selective than many writers. Rothstein's approach allows the fullest assessment of the patient's transference, the patient's resistance, and the therapist's countertransference. He omits any stringent selection process and views the assessment as the work of analysis, starting from the first session. Psychotherapists not trained to conduct formal analysis might still use the same principle. Analytically oriented psychotherapy has typically been viewed as making fewer demands on the patient in terms of rigor and ego strength, as well as having less comprehensive goals. If the psychotherapist were to take most patients as potential candidates for treatment and pursue the understanding and analysis of the transference, albeit in a less comprehensive manner, then the early assessments could focus on the symptoms, their meanings, and the development of a suitable working relationship. What Rothstein seeks in his assessment and early interventions is an analytic collaboration. The aim of assessment in the first session, then, is to find whether a collaboration between therapist and patient can be established, regardless of the diagnosis of the patient.

Some important assessment decisions must be made by the therapist in the early sessions of psychotherapy. These are best kept to a minimum and are aimed at creating an atmosphere void of treatment decisions and within which the work of exploration can occur, unencumbered by urgency to act. It is this stance of analysis, rather than of action, that is crucial to the work of long-term therapy. Actions lend themselves to *acting out*, a term that has been sorely damaged by popular misuse. The technical meaning of the term refers to the patient's enactment of the transference rather than the raising of unconscious material through the flow of free associations. For example, the patient fails to remember a long-established appointment as his associations approach some feeling of anger or eroticism toward the analyst. This acting out can then be used in the treatment, but it moves the patient out of the arena of interpretation and understanding for a time.

Similarly, countertransference feelings can be acted out by the therapist. These might even take the form of treatment decisions that remove the therapist from a position of understanding and using those feelings in the treatment. An example occurred in my practice. A man called seeking an appointment. He stated in the phone call that he had seen another therapist in town for some time and was no longer going to work with that therapist. He was interested in entering therapy with me and he requested that I obtain records from the other therapist before our first meeting. I asked why that seemed important to him and he quickly replied that he did not want to go through all of that again, he wanted to start working on other things. In the awkwardness of the phone conversation and the seeming urgency of his request I agreed to obtain the records. This is not my usual practice and it is even a practice I avoid. I hope to hear what a new patient has to say untainted by anyone else's interpretations. I was able to reconsider this experience and I ultimately did not obtain the records. Obtaining records is a common activity in the mental health field; it is often considered a part of a thorough assessment and today it is even recommended as a matter of course for therapists as a protection from liability exposure (Hedges et al. 1997). I could easily rationalize my change of practice, which I did in the pressure of the first phone call. But that action was a countertransference response to a patient's urgency and to the unexamined "need" for me to have these records. It ultimately became clear that this man was very frightened of my reaction to what was written about him by his previous therapist and the request for the records was a way of testing whether or not I could tolerate him or would abort the therapy before beginning. This self-deprecation was then a major theme of the ongoing treatment.

Schafer (1983) has stated that the analyst *analyzes*. From the outset of therapy the therapist must have this stance, even in the task of initial assessments. The therapist's constraint is important in the face of the patient's unconscious pull for action. This can occur in subtle and initially unrecognizable ways. One writer (Anderson 1998) describes a series of requests by her patient, all of them "reasonable," but in their reasonableness drawing the therapist into an enactment that ultimately must be analyzed. Another skilled and experienced therapist described to me the request of a patient to come see her house. The therapist was experienced in psychodynamic treatment and realized that for the woman some important meanings were linked to this house. But, caught for a moment by the way the patient asked and some other quality, likely unconscious, the therapist replied that she could not do that. This reply, one assuming an action was necessary, injured the patient and temporarily derailed the exploration of what her house meant. The therapist lost her stance of analysis over action and was drawn into a transference enactment. In assessment and especially in the earliest stages of therapy the tendency to this can be great.

This balance between assessment and assessment decisions is a critical aspect of setting a stage for the development of the transference. As we become increasingly responsible for rapidly assessing and reporting child abuse and elder abuse, quickly ascertaining the reality of suicidal or homicidal ideas, making accurate decisions regarding physiological illnesses, deciding on the need for medicines, and making appropriate referrals, the confidentiality of psychotherapy is eroded and the primary focus of the therapist is disrupted. Even when perfectly accurate assessment decisions are made they can disrupt and even derail the psychotherapeutic process. Psychotherapy ought to be started in a way that best demonstrates that the work will involve a careful exploration of one's feelings, without urgency to act or decide. This stance is in contrast to the growing number of mandated acts the psychotherapist must perform.

Slowing the Action

Analytic therapies have historically emphasized slowing the process, delaying decisions and action, and allowing for the most thorough exploration possible between two people. This is the atmosphere the therapist is trying to approach. Even the very minuscule assessment decisions that occur in the course of treatment, the decisions to interpret or intervene, are decisions that at least temporarily interrupt the patient's experiencing. Each interpretation at least momentarily stops the flow of exploration. A patient some distance into treatment became agitated by overhearing a voice through the wall of my office. The words were not audible, but the tone of the person's voice was shrill and penetrated the soundproofing. My patient reacted but was reluctant to speak about what was bothering her. I assumed she was annoyed by the noise. In what I later understood to be a countertransference enactment of my frustrations with her seeming resistance to speak of her feelings and associations, I remarked about her unwillingness to express her upset with me and my office. She did not respond, and left the session without revealing more. In the following session this patient went on to tell me about her associations, which I had been too impatient to wait for in the previous session. She remembered her parents arguing, threatening each other, and then all the sound stopping. She gave me more details, but it became clear then that she had become terrified in the previous session, recalling a childhood terror of finding some horrible scene upon leaving her bedroom. Then, she had remained silent until the next morning, fearing what she would see, silent just as she had been at my proddings in the session. The further exploration, temporarily interrupted only by my efforts at interpretation, proved much more fruitful than my earlier speculation. Only an analytic stance that allows for the unrestricted exploration of meanings can achieve this experience between the patient and therapist.

The task of assessment in the first session is constrained by the nature of the atmosphere that must be created for the therapist to conduct analytic therapy. A confrontive assessment, an authoritative interview, a psychometric test that implies x-ray-like precision, all obstruct the development of an analytic collaboration. Assessments that aim at decisions begin to conflict with the analytic ideal of careful, unfettered exploration of one's inner life.

Another pressure to act rather than analyze may arise as an effect of how much the therapist knows from his skill in reading and interpreting the unconscious. We can observe and conjecture about a person and even draw reasonably accurate conclusions very quickly. Therapists can make many reasonable speculations that are borne out over the course of time. However, it is not useful to convey all of this information as soon as we have it. In fact as therapists we may have to wait a long time to use the information or wait a long time for it to be understandable to the patient.

Winnicott (1971) warns the therapist against being too clever, underscoring the importance of letting the patient find her way in the telling of her story. He realizes how much more the therapist knows and how clever and insightful that can sound, and also the detrimental effect it might have on the patient's growth toward autonomy. The work of therapy is not about the delivery of information; that is education. Therapy is about the use of an unconscious process for the patient's growth and well-being.

The following sections discuss common methods of assessment in an effort to distill out what is most useful in the first
session of analytic therapy. Psychotherapy may be thought of as
beginning with a trial and the focus of that trial will be what I call
a *micro-assessment* of the interaction between the therapist and
patient. A micro-assessment captures the essential first-session
assessments. I discuss certain symptoms that I have met in the
first session and that I imagine are common and frustrating to
many therapists. Finally, assessment of the patient is only one of
the four assessment perspectives that begin in the first session and
continue through the treatment. The common assessment is the
therapist's assessment of the patient. Three others are often
overlooked: the therapist's self assessment, the patient's assessment of the therapist, and the patient's self assessment.

METHODS, MEANS, AND GOALS

All of the many techniques of assessment inform the psychotherapist's work, but none can simply be applied to the first
session. Some methods of assessment may even impede the
development of a psychotherapeutic process. In traditional techniques of assessment the mental health professional is the expert
observing and drawing conclusions about the patient. This
model, in which diagnosis precedes treatment, may start a
psychotherapy off with a skewed sense of who will do what and
how the process is going to proceed.

Conventions in the mental health field and current methods of
psychological assessment may incline us to think that assessment
of the patient can be an adequate predictor of how that patient
will fare with any competent therapist. In actuality it can only be
said that this individual might exhibit these characteristic conflicts or difficulties and so certain themes might be anticipated in
the therapeutic relationship. One cannot predict how a particular
patient will react and relate to a particular therapist; there are too
many variables. Even were it possible to account for all the
variables, as in mapping the genes of DNA, such prediction
might still be undesirable. We may best leave such selections up

to the patient's choice and then analyze the resulting relationship. If the goal is to judge the potential success of the treatment
we must instead consider the relationship. The assessments
necessary in a first session and in early sessions of a treatment are
what I call *micro-assessment*. Micro-assessment (discussed at
length later in this chapter), is less concerned with categories of
diagnosis and more focused on the intricacies of the transference
and countertransference themes of two individuals in the first
session.

Psychological Testing

Psychological testing, whether extensive or brief, involves the use
of some form of standardized device, researched for validity and
reliability of measurement. The advent and growth of psychological testing is a critical piece of the establishment of psychology as a profession, and the use of tests has greatly advanced our
ability to assess the human personality for many purposes. Not
the least of these purposes is the work of research on the methods
and treatments of psychotherapy. In clinics and institutions the
use of psychological testing as part of pre- and post-assessments
of treatment has expanded the understanding of psychotherapy.
The research demand, however, is recognized as an intrusion on
the treatment, since often such projects are conducted with clinic
patients who receive treatment for a reduced fee. The competent
researcher also recognizes the influence of the measurement
techniques on the outcome of the research and the treatment.
Formal assessments, especially those using devices and psycho-
metrics, are understood to be an intrusion on the therapy.
Perhaps researchers recognize in this that while they help the
overall development and advancement of therapy for all patients,
the requirements of the research do not directly help the patient,
and may intrude on the work devoted to that end.

A psychotherapist could greet each patient with a battery of
psychometric tests, even send the potential patient home with
the tests or send them to a patient before the first session. No
doubt a great deal of information could be gathered from the

testing and many speculations made. Presumably treatment could proceed from what is found. But we must ask what the patient would experience from such an approach. The use of tests and forms at the outset may create an undesirable expectation in the patient. Some patients familiar with medical techniques may wait passively for the results of testing and expect that like an x-ray the diagnosis will be certain and the treatment carried out without the patient's involvement. (Even x-rays are not the objective diagnostic methods we are inclined to suppose they are, otherwise we would not need highly trained radiologists to interpret them.) This is not the impression an analytic therapist wishes to create in a first session, or any session for that matter. The effect on the patient must inform our use of such techniques.

Patient History

In order to conduct any psychotherapy some history must be obtained. Some advocate a formal history taking, and contemporary psychology, with all of its attention to fair disclosure and liability, even advocates an extensive form that requests all manner of information from the patient. In many cases the patient is asked to fill out this form prior to being able to speak about her complaints. Information is obtained by these methods, but it is all self-reported by the patient and therefore contaminated by all of the problems associated with self-report inventories. The simple report forms made by individual therapists are not validated as psychometric instruments and thus have no more predictive value than what is gained in talking to the therapist. But, most important, with a form all of the crucial information and observations of how the patient reports his experiences is lost, along with all that can be obtained from the therapist's experience of the patient's moods, nonverbal communications, projections, and affects. Similarly, the patient loses the experience of the therapist's empathic communication as he reports the complaints and troubles that motivated the request for therapy.

The patient's history, development, family, current life situation, and specific history of the presenting complaint often take up a formalized or structured part of a diagnostic or intake interview. I once saw a twelve-page form, in 10-point type, single spaced, that was used by a psychologist to gather initial historical information on new patients. What is the patient's experience of all of this? Such a form seemed more a test of the person's stamina than a useful way to gather necessary information and initiate the process of a long-term psychotherapy relationship.

In contrast, in my earliest days of learning psychotherapy I tried very hard to be an analyst as I best I understood that from observation and reading. To that end I worked from the fantasy that analysts only speak to make an interpretation; they most certainly do not ask questions. This greatly inhibited my manner of taking on a new patient. Obviously I also failed in the most basic courtesies of meeting this new person: I was too silent, too mimicking of a caricature I had of the analyst in my mind. Likely some of this experience has spawned this book. The clinician with the form described above, however, seeks too much information in the beginning, imitating an attorney or a detective, and not the empathic listening of an analytic therapist.

The diagnostic interview is a specialized technique that is valuable and important in psychiatry and psychology. It is a structured interview in which the clinician is intent upon establishing a working diagnosis for purposes of research, treatment, or forensic decisions. Diagnosis in this instance usually refers to a diagnosis from *The Diagnostic and Statistical Manual* (*DSM*), a categorization of an individual that is broadly related to clusters of symptoms that can be observed in a particular situation or period of time. We are trained to make these kinds of diagnoses, but again the question arises as to whether this sort of diagnosis, especially if made in a first session, is of any great significance to the continuation of a psychoanalytic psychotherapy.

DIAGNOSIS—SOME THOUGHTS AND CONSIDERATIONS

In large part the diagnosis is not for the patient. Having a diagnosis assigned will not lessen the patient's suffering and will not benefit the patient in some direct way. Diagnosis has a variety of purposes that serve the treatment of the patient, but it is not directly linked to the relief of suffering in the patient or to the analysis of the patient's conflicts. There are three layers of usefulness to a diagnosis for psychotherapy. The least important is the administrative need for one. This is the use of diagnosis for billing insurance providers or for clinic records that are used for statistical analysis of patient populations. Typically this use requires only a code number or diagnostic name. Increasingly, insurers are requiring reporting of each *DSM* axis of the diagnosis, presumably so that progress in treatment can be measured, and no doubt so that treatment can be limited. Now insurers are also requiring extensive supportive observations and ongoing reports. This serves patients in that it enables them to obtain their benefits; it does not serve patients in that their privacy is eroded. The reporting does not advance the understanding of diagnostic categories or actually direct the treatment. Often, reports are written to continue benefits, not to improve treatment.

Diagnoses and codes create an interesting interaction with the patient. Most patients do not even know to ask about diagnosis until the first billing takes place. Of course mental-health students in treatment are always aware of this need and are both eager and frightened to find out their diagnosis. The diagnosis must be given to the insurance company and often the patient sees this paperwork. Some therapists have shown reluctance to let the patient know this piece of information. First, the information is immediately available to the patient through the insurer. Second, if the therapist only uses the *DSM* code, leaving out the diagnostic name as if to fool the patient, the patient need only go to the library and look up the category. Meanwhile an area of secrecy has been placed between patient and therapist and something secret about the patient has been established that may lead to all sorts of difficulty in the future. It is further troubling that this secret from the patient is one to be kept between the therapist and someone else, outside of the therapy office. Negative results of such a stance will certainly enter into the treatment. Therapy is a treatment that relies on honesty. The therapist's dishonesty to the patient or to an outside agency only presents a conflicting message about the work.

A second function of diagnosis that has a bit more importance in the patient's treatment is its use in professional communications, such as making a referral. If the referral is made to another psychotherapist for treatment we often give a tentative diagnosis presumably to indicate something of what the therapist might expect. However, that therapist must and will make her own assessment; the diagnosis is a courtesy, not a necessity. One might just as well say, "I am sending Ms. Smith to you for treatment. She has just gone through a divorce and is feeling quite at a loss with herself." If the therapist is sending a patient for an adjunctive treatment such as medication evaluation, the diagnosis once again is a courtesy; the physician making the evaluation must make her own assessment, both for reasons of liability as well as the ethics of seeing the person face to face. This purpose of diagnosis is professional, and serves the patient in only a distant way. It does serve the professional and perhaps has a statistical and research purpose related to psychotherapy.

The third use of diagnosis is the most directly related to the work of psychotherapy. Kernberg (1984) has been the most thoroughgoing in the development of a diagnostic picture in an extended first session. Eissler and colleagues (1977) developed a diagnostic profile that was detailed and comprehensive and described the patient in an ego psychology framework. Their format was not to be used directly with the patient; rather it was for the therapist's use and would be updated as treatment proceeded.

Each of these methods involves the careful assessment of a patient from a psychoanalytic perspective with a view to understanding the presenting concerns of the patient and directing a course of treatment. Every psychotherapist does well to understand the basic ideas here. Most psychotherapists probably have some personal categories into which they organize their understanding of a patient. For the initial interview, Kernberg's (1984) method is more systematic—it follows a more medical model in which diagnosis precedes treatment—but the underlying thrust is to get a beginning picture of the patient in order to make assessment decisions about the appropriate treatment.

Kernberg's (1984) use of diagnosis is far broader than code number and category. He is pursuing a thorough picture of that individual's psychodynamics, much as Eissler and colleagues (1977) are. Kernberg was making treatment decisions in the setting in which he offered this procedure, and he stood by a selection process that directed a patient to psychotherapy or other treatments and perhaps with a therapist different than the assessor. Eissler and colleagues (1977) were more interested in providing a framework for the therapist to use over time as a way of formulating understanding of the patient without necessarily directing decisions.

"Fit" and Patient–Therapist Matching

A trial of psychotherapy, several sessions to assess whether this therapist and this patient can work well enough together, is the basis of micro-assessment. It is impossible to predict which patient will succeed with which therapist. Nonetheless, most patients sincerely seeking psychotherapy will probably make a pretty good go of it with a competent therapist. The important point here is that it must be left up to the therapist and the patient to determine whether this relationship is worth pursuing. Each of the individuals involved will have a private assessment of the fit.

A recent phenomenon in current practice is an effort at patient–therapist matching. Perhaps this has always gone on in some way or other. A referring therapist tries to make a fit more likely. I doubt that there have ever been any clear guidelines to how this is done, except, of course, personal theory and intuition. I am speaking of something unrelated to skill, as any referring therapist will send a very difficult or very needy patient to the most skilled therapist that can be had. I am referring here to matching a therapist for gender, sexual orientation, religious preference, ethnic background, or some other social criteria. The growing use of this approach to making referrals has undermined the therapist's expertise.

First of all, making referrals in this way is seldom based in any research or theory. It is unlikely that any research could ever control for all of the variables at work in such matching, no more than for any attempt to assess the potential success of a therapy relationship. Yet we go on trying to send the patient to just the right therapist. The most important problem with such a technique is that it fails to take account of the most critical variables in analytic therapy, the unconscious ones. Gender, sexual orientation, and religious preference are only surface indications of one's underlying conflicts or personality structure, not very substantial measures for the proposed matching. Also, to specify all of this information about the therapist is an intrusion into the therapist's personal life and privacies. Contemporary analytic therapists are looking carefully at self-disclosure of the therapist's privacies. But this refers to the clinical use of self-disclosure, not the "outing" of a colleague in the process of referral.

This has all led to the worst aspect of patient–therapist matching. Since mental-health professionals have freely engaged in such matching and have failed to teach the public what might actually matter in selecting a therapist, the public now expects it. I have heard all manner of requests. One couple asked for a therapist who had a teenage son with the same diagnosis as their child. Another potential patient "needed" a male therapist, never divorced, who was a practicing Catholic. These questions from a patient used to be taken up as evidence of fears to be explored or concerns worthy of analysis. Today mental-health professionals are more inclined to make such an assessment decision, or, to speak plainly, to accept out of hand the assessment decision of the patient.

This is not to say that the patient's request is to be ignored. We cannot help an individual come to a place of self-assessment if as therapists we override the patient's feelings, fears, and experience with authority. Patients must be guided to make self-assessments and choices even in the first session or the phone call. But we are most helpful if we do not collude with an unfounded means of selecting a therapist. Fears and wishes deserve careful, empathic analysis, even by the referring therapist. As we return to this sort of referral, to competent, professional psychotherapists, with empathy for the patient's fears and concerns, the public might again see us as experts, begin to understand the actual needs for therapy, and experience the way therapy helps even from the contact with the referring professional.

Freud on Assessment

Freud's assessment of the human personality constitutes the core of his writings about the analysis and understanding of human dynamics. Having particular pertinence to the beginning of psychoanalysis are his ideas as captured in two papers, "Notes Upon a Case of Obsessional Neurosis" (1909), which includes the first session of the man called Rat Man, and "On Psychotherapy" (1904), in which he describes his criteria of analyzability. Freud selected those individuals who could form a transference and ultimately experience a transference neurosis with the analyst. He presumed that psychotic patients and those with certain character disorders would not succeed, though he was hopeful for an expansion of analytic techniques that would someday achieve a form of treatment suitable to a wider range of patients. That, of course, has occurred.

Since Freud was intently focused on the analysis of the patient's transference, and especially oedipal dynamics, his recommendations all aim at establishing the best possible environment for its development. Part of Freud's motivation for establishing stringent selection criteria was that he was seeking to get psychoanalysis recognized as a scientifically based treatment, one respected by the medical community. He could not afford to have disgruntled patients running about or many failures that could be cited by detractors. His criteria aimed at a certain segment of the population. Those patients needed to be reasonably well educated, of good character, and nonpsychotic. Specifically, patients had to be suffering from psychoneurosis—those he believed to be likely to use the treatment successfully and to be able to manage the rigors of the work.

Further setting the stage for analysis of transference and for beginning treatment, and making it possible to have a trial analysis, Freud (1913) suggested some criteria for judging what would make analysis possible. He warned against patients who did not show motivation for treatment that arose from their own suffering. Those sent to treatment by others, presumably spouses (and today we might include the courts and treatment programs), would not have sufficient motivation to sustain treatment. He then warned of prior contact between the patient and the analyst, and even of the effects of prior treatment. In these cases, a transference was pre-formed and would make the early stages of analysis more difficult. Ellman (1991) notes that in contemporary practice this last criterion might be almost impossible to apply, since many patients are not naive to treatment but have had significant prior experience. It is likely that contemporary understanding of the transference and the analysis of it are advanced to a point that a pre-formed transference is not so disturbing to later work as Freud felt. Numerous writers have in fact explored psychotherapy as a preparation to analysis (Horowitz 1990, Levine et al 1983), actually encouraging prior psychotherapy experience. Most important is the acknowledgment of the prior experience and the therapist's recognition of the effects of that experience. Today, the understanding of transference is broader; moreover, since analyses and psychotherapy now extend much longer than in Freud's day there is adequate time to analyze the many threads in the transference.

Trial Analysis

Perhaps more difficult for the start of therapy is prior contact between therapist and patient. This refers mostly to professional contact, but Freud (1913) noted that if one set out to analyze a friend he must be prepared to lose that friend. He also warned of engaging in lengthy consultations prior to analysis. These are nonanalytic beginnings, and he felt them to be unproductive. From these recommendations he emphasized the trial of analysis as the best method of making an assessment about whether a patient was suitable. For patients one does not have any information about, Freud (1913) suggests a two-week trial, so that not too much is invested on the part of either patient or analyst if it is not going to work. But one must understand that this allowed a significant degree of assessment, since Freud met his patients for six sixty-minute sessions per week. Today some managed-care insurers do not even allow that much time for an entire treatment.

The trial then provided both Freud and the patient with the best experience of analysis, an actual experience. Freud recommended that the trial proceed with no change in the rules of treatment. I believe that the most important aspect of the trial is that the work of analysis or of psychotherapy cannot be conveyed to the patient cognitively or intellectually: it must be experienced. The consultation and the education about analysis may all be valuable, but they do not demonstrate the technique and they do not allow for the spontaneous experience of the transference by both therapist and patient.

Freud's method is colored by his intention to bring respect to the psychoanalytic treatment as well as the infancy of the technique itself. Today psychoanalytic psychotherapy is more fully developed and widely practiced, but Freud's recommendations still have merit for psychotherapy. A trial of psychotherapy is an even more suitable method of assessment, especially if the psychotherapist has the resources to provide or refer to adjunctive treatments such as medication evaluation, hospitalization, and other forms of case management. The therapist can begin outpatient treatment, even with a very disturbed patient, knowing that more extensive forms of containment can be initiated if necessary. Freud's specific criteria for the patient—education, reasonable character, nonpsychotic—are too narrow given the widening scope of patients accepted and the less constraining parameters to psychotherapeutic treatment.

Many of Freud's other recommendations remain especially useful. One example is the growing concern with dual relationships, instances in which the therapist has a role in the patient's life outside of the therapy. This is an area where therapists tend to get into trouble. The widening variety of patients who seek therapy and are deemed suitable has in fact opened treatment to more troubled individuals who are more likely to have disturbances in the area of ego boundaries. Their treatment is a valuable advancement of psychoanalytic technique, but it places a growing burden on the therapist. In this environment, the importance of clarity about boundaries from the beginning of treatment is even more important. Freud's recommendation is a good starting guideline and sufficient numbers of competent therapists exist in most places that one need not begin a therapy relationship that constitutes a dual relationship.

The psychotherapist working analytically is as intent as Freud was on allowing the transference to emerge and using it to the patient's benefit. All of the efforts and guidelines aimed toward creating a proper environment apply equally to the psychotherapist. The trial of psychotherapy, starting the treatment just as it will proceed in the future, is the most likely to create such an atmosphere.

That the patient seeking treatment must be motivated by her own suffering is an important part of the assessment as well as an important element in whether or not the therapy will proceed. I will discuss this aspect of the assessment under micro-assessment, later in this chapter, but Freud rightly noted that patients coerced or otherwise manipulated to treatment do not make much use of it. The psychotherapist may make some inroads to the patient who presents as unmotivated on the surface, if, in fact, there is some significant underlying pain to motivate the person to stay with the treatment over time.

Psychotherapy offered in outpatient private practices is most likely begun with a trial. There may be no formal shift to ongoing therapy, but just a gradual unspoken understanding. The patient may be the one to end the trial. Patients feel relief from the initial symptoms and choose to cease treatment at that point, even in the face of the best efforts of the therapist. They have proven themselves to be unsuitable at that time for continued treatment. Yet some do return and use the initial positive experience to seek treatment at a later time when their suffering is not so easily resisted. The therapist open to treating a wide range of patients may best begin each therapy with a trial. Some therapists call the first session a consultation, emphasizing that it is a time for both therapist and patient to assess if this is a treatment and relationship each wishes to pursue. In this way the first and several more sessions become a trial of therapy, and the therapist, like Freud, will want the patient to experience the treatment as it will occur many sessions hence.

OVERLOOKED ASSESSMENTS

The discussion above relates to the therapist's careful assessment of the patient's personality dynamics, the fit between patient and therapist, the realistic issues of whether the patient is able to engage in treatment with this therapist given the costs and scheduling demands, and the degree of containment this patient will require—that is, whether psychotherapy in an outpatient office is possible for this patient. This is the emphasis of assessment, and the focus of a therapist's training is placed on this aspect of assessment. In fact, therapists probably have more information and ability to make an assessment than can ever be conveyed to a patient in a first session or in many later sessions. But other assessments are inherent in the first session and throughout the therapy. Each deserves attention because these assessments too begin in the first session. These are also perspectives seldom discussed in the overall topic of assessment for psychotherapy.

The Patient's Assessment of the Therapist

In a first session, the potential patient is making an assessment of the therapist. Therapists may not like the patient's methods, or like the feeling of being "shopped"; they may not like the criteria the patient uses to assess the therapist, but the fact of the patient's assessment of the therapist cannot be ignored. The therapist's failure to meet the patient's expectations may abort the therapy.

The patient's capability to assess the therapist in a useful manner is certainly affected and impaired by the conflicts and dynamics that will eventually become the subject of the therapy. In the first session the therapist must observe the patient's methods, try to raise the patient's thoughts about the assessment into view, and begin to explore with the patient the way he is making an assessment. The therapist gets a beginning picture of many characteristics of the patient in this process and the patient gets a beginning picture of how the therapist works.

A sensitive understanding of the patient's efforts at assessment helps to convey to the patient that the therapist respects the patient's autonomy. This is a very confused area in the mental health field as well as the medical field. Perhaps a long history of physician and psychotherapist authoritarianism has created a skeptical public. The public is encouraged to question the doctor, to gain information and education about treatments, and in general to be better informed. These are valuable patient skills and the health care field rightly responds. However, psychotherapy aims at the growth of a person's autonomy and responsibility, and the misunderstanding and misuse of this newfound patient attitude has resulted in an attitude to the patient as a kind of customer: "the patient is always right." This is misdirected and incorrect. In health care as in psychotherapy the doctor does, in fact, have an expertise that the patient cannot gain simply by asserting autonomy over health-care issues. Autonomy and choice do not translate into patient expertise.

The distinction here is between authority and authoritarianism and between knowing what is in a patient's mind and knowing how to treat the patient's mind. There is a historical authoritarianism in psychoanalysis in which the presumption has been that the doctor-analyst knows better than the patient. No doubt this attitude is reflected in the medical profession and has stimulated the public questioning of doctors. But an air of authoritarianism does not help the process of psychotherapy, since the patient's partnership in discovering the inner workings of the mind is essential. The therapist knows how to treat these conflicts in the mind and how to discern them in the emerging transference. This is the therapist's authority and the therapist will require some conditions in order to carry on that treatment adequately. But fostering the illusion that one knows the state of the patient's mind or what is in the patient's mind impedes discovery and stimulates negative reactions in many patients today. Shor (1992) is quite clear about his intention to help the patient discover her own mind, values, and private workings—matters about which

the patient is the authority. Mitchell (1998) analyzes the underlying changes in philosophy that have adjusted many contemporary therapists' ideas of authority. He concludes that the therapist
is an authority about how to conduct the collaboration for the
patient's self reflection, but not an authority on what is in the
patient's mind.

The patient's method of assessing the therapist must be
understood within the context of respect for what the patient
feels and knows in his own mind, and the fact that the therapist
knows best how an analytic collaboration can develop and
proceed. The patient's assessment of the therapist will be influenced by important transference themes. The therapist's task will
be to cull the patient's experience and ideas and begin to make
use of them in an analytic manner while maintaining respect and
empathy for the patient's experience. The patient's assessments
of the therapist that will initially threaten the possibility of
therapy are negative transference themes, which will arise early
with some patients. In some cases these are ready-made transferences, the powerful attitudes that a patient might have before
ever experiencing much of the therapist. The societal attitude of
entitlement that supports the stance of patient-more-expert-
than-doctor may be the supporting rationale for this.

Patients' assessments of the therapist are like all associations
and productions in therapy—in need of understanding and
exploration. The notion that the therapist wants to initially and
immediately quell is that simple "feelings," and the conclusions
the patient draws from those feelings, are to be acted on; rather,
these are the subject of the therapy. All therapists have heard
these early expectations from patients relatively naive to therapy.
A patient asks, "Do you give feedback? I can't sit with a therapist
who doesn't talk." Another says, "I won't pay for sessions I miss,
I think that's dishonest and I won't tolerate it." These "assessments" probably arise from some past therapy experience or the
discussed experience of another. The analytic therapist's answer is
not, "Of course I give feedback," or "I won't (or will) insist on
you paying for missed sessions," because these questions are
openings to begin the work of therapy and to demonstrate how
such concerns will be handled in the future.

A colleague told me this example. A man called and specifically asked for psychoanalytic psychotherapy. The therapist presumed some familiarity with treatment to ask so specifically. Some time into the session the patient asked the therapist if he believed in God. The experienced analytic therapist began a process of trying to move the patient's question to an analytic exploration. He queried what the patient might be anxious about, what the question meant to him, and so on. On this point the patient was relentless and insisted that he could go no further unless he knew that his therapist believed in God. Many therapists in a first session would see this as the end. Some therapists would answer the question but anticipate later conflict with a supervisor. The therapist responded that analytic psychotherapy involved the exploration of underlying ideas and feelings, not the simple response to any question that arose, and since this man had asked for such treatment, wouldn't it be more on track to pursue the meaning of this question? I believe the man continued. The therapist did not reject the man's concern, he did not answer the man's question, nor did he start the therapy on a track where analytic therapy does not go. He gently took the man's concern and attempted to move to an exploration. He persisted in this, backing up to educate the man a bit about what he was doing, and created the germ of an analytic collaboration.

In psychotherapy, unlike other professions, the patient's experience is a crucial aspect of the work and of the ultimate success of the therapy. An attorney can accomplish his task for the client whether or not the client has a good experience of the attorney. Patients come to us already assessing their experience of the therapist, and all of their personality and projections come into play. Sometimes a patient makes those associations available for immediate analysis and contact, but often these are left unspoken for a time; if the patient stays, these may be analyzed or the patient may simply leave to discuss the failure of fit with another therapist.

The Therapist's Self-Assessment

Psychoanalysis has placed great importance on the therapist's self-understanding, and the therapist's analysis or personal psy-

chotherapy has always been a crucial aspect of training in the
practice of psychotherapy. While some would describe their
analysis or psychotherapy as a training exercise, the honest
therapist is aware of the personal nature of one's own therapy and
the necessity of gaining clarity about one's own conflicts and
unconscious motivations. Personal therapy and a perpetual self-
reflection in the course of the practice of psychotherapy are what
make the analytic therapist an instrument of the treatment,
capable of withstanding and using the intense power of the
patient's transference. They are also what make the career of
psychotherapy particularly rewarding; the therapist is constantly
stimulated to grow and expand her inner world, challenged by
the patient's demands as well as the value of ongoing self-
analysis.

Ethics codes place their emphasis on a therapist's competence
to treat a certain patient. This is a broad statement of self-
assessment, one which is less important to the present discussion.
But it should be noted that the therapist does bear such a
responsibility and one must keep aware of areas of needed
theoretical knowledge, consultation, and supervision, of the level
of training one has attained, and of whether a given case requires
certain special training in order for one to be competent to treat.
An example here might be the area of eating disorders. In the
most severe presentation of an eating disorder it is frequently
necessary to have medical support, since the patient's life is often
in danger. This may require certain knowledge additional to the
therapist's usual skills and competence in general psychotherapy.
I am of the opinion, however, that analytic therapists are by
training skilled to treat the personality and that not every
symptom presentation necessarily requires a specialization. The
field of mental health is inclined to require specialty knowledge
of symptoms, sometimes to the neglect of human personality
development. This area is not, in fact, a first-session issue so
much as an issue for any therapist in practice who must define in
advance what he is qualified to do. I believe that the analytic
therapist is qualified to treat a wide range of symptom disorders
because the treatment is one of uncovering the hidden personality issues.

Ethics codes address the conscious actions of a therapist against a patient. From an analytic perspective of further concern to the competent treatment of the patient are the actions of the therapist motivated by his unanalyzed conflicts. Ethics focus on training and the cognitive skills of the therapist, but the analytic stance elevates the therapist's personal psychotherapy as an equally important factor in preparing him for the work. Not only will that experience give the therapist awareness of his own dynamics, but the therapist's successful experience will be the foundation of bringing a hopeful and valuable experience to the patient's therapy.

My concern about the therapist's self-assessment for the first session has to do with the earliest threads of countertransference. The question I want to be asking myself in a first session has to do with how I respond to this patient. Some have discussed this from the aspect of whether the therapist "likes" the patient, I think in an effort to get into very basic feelings and experiences of the therapist. This also raises the point that we are not required to treat every patient who enters our offices, and that selection is in the best interests of both patient and therapist. Rothstein (1990) discusses this at some length. His technique, especially in the first session, is to take all of these subjective feelings as indications of countertransference. In this he begins the therapy as an analytic one, and is bent on understanding the meanings of all the experience the patient brings to it. It is not important whether the therapist likes or dislikes the patient, but that this experience can be understood in its deepest meaning. What Rothstein counts as most important is whether the therapist and patient can establish an analytic collaboration around whatever feelings arise in the beginnings of the treatment.

The therapist's self-assessment takes place on several different levels. Regarding issues of the contract, the therapist must assess whether or not to engage in a contract with this patient, given the fee and scheduling requirements. If the therapist feels compelled in some way to take this patient on, straining the therapist's needs for income or a regular schedule, then perhaps further assessment of one's countertransference is in order. The realistic matters of fee and schedule may be influenced both by demands from the patient and the therapist's own dynamics of caretaking, rescuing, or difficulties with limits. Often the assessment has to do more directly with countertransference trends, not well formulated at the first moments of treatment, and involves such questions as "What does this patient stir in my feelings?" or "Am I drawn into what this person tells me?" or "Do I feel the energy and enthusiasm necessary to begin a new therapy and with this particular patient?" or "Do I understand what this person is telling me?" or "Is there something about this person's dynamics that potentially inhibits my ability to work with him?" For example, I am interested if the new patient causes an inner reaction in me that could be used to further understanding over time. A patient who causes an experience of boredom or distance in the therapist may be very difficult to start with, or to get to a place where the roots of those experiences can be adequately analyzed. I know from my experience of doing therapy that very often patients who harbor feelings of rage that are strongly defended against tend to make me drowsy. It is sometimes difficult for me to work through that experience in a way that is useful to the patient and without my offending the patient with my apparent lack of interest.

The new patient must also be understandable to the therapist, even at the superficial level of language. Some patients for whom English is not a first language can be difficult for the English-speaking therapist to understand because of their accent. Here the questions are, "How much difficulty will this create over time?" and "Is this an indication that cultural differences will make the understanding even more problematic?" Even when therapist and patient share a first language there are potential difficulties in use of vocabulary, or a requirement that perhaps the therapist speak in a way that is not customary, for example using simple language for a less-educated patient, that might be difficult and tedious over time.

Some of the above issues concern basic considerations of communication. The therapist's self-assessment must consider whether the patient will be understandable even at this level. Further issues involve what might be considered the therapist's transference reactions. The therapist must assess what patient presentations and personalities will cause her special difficulties. For example, I described above the female therapist who rightly refused to treat a male perpetrator of sexual abuse because she was repulsed by the man's act to the extent that she could not honestly work for that person's goals and best interests. The therapist who tends to be drawn into the helpless feelings of a needy, poorly functioning person may be cautious in taking on persons of that sort, who capture the therapist's unconscious transference reactions.

The Patient's Self-Assessment

Even in a first session a patient is making self-assessments. In the simplest way the patient is monitoring anxiety, reflecting on the experience with this therapist, and determining how much to say and what can be tolerated from the other person. Each patient will do this with varying degrees of skill and success. The patient's capacity for self-assessment is actually the subject of the psychotherapy. Like the capability for self-assessment the therapist has gained in personal therapy, this is the broad goal of therapy for the patient. It is one part of the assessment that begins in the first session.

The therapist's assessment of the patient will take account of how well the patient can make self-assessments. The therapist queries, "What was it like for you, growing up?" The patient replies, "It was all good" or "I had a very loving mother" or "I was constantly terrified" or "I don't remember"—all self-assessments that may prove accurate or not over time, though each is already giving a clue as to the nature of the patient's self-understanding.

From the outset the therapist is guiding the patient to more successful self-assessment. Rather than endorsing the patient's initial self-assessment, the work of therapy consists in demonstrating the value of a more thorough analysis of that experience and in leading the patient away from action toward self-reflection. The therapist is not making the patient's assessment, but conducting the therapy in a way that allows the patient to develop a richer understanding of the experience she is assessing.

MICRO-ASSESSMENT

The first session of psychotherapy is a single defined portion of what will become an ongoing process that will continue until termination. More important than diagnosis or the development of a complete picture of the patient or even a conclusive determination about what might occur in therapy, the first session has an assessment focus: that is, the unique and idiosyncratic relationship of one therapist and one patient. This process, as mentioned earlier, I call micro-assessment.

The analytic therapist must engage the patient's involvement from the outset. The therapist has no authenticity scales or honesty measures that operate without the patient's assistance. The therapist needs a patient who is motivated by his suffering to seek treatment and who is able to begin to enter a process toward relief. In the opening phase of treatment both patient and therapist must establish an analytic collaboration in which each plays a part. The potential for this collaboration and the dynamics that will ensue are the subject of micro-assessment.

Assessment in the first session is not focused on diagnosis. For me, administrative diagnosis is of no concern, and, if the patient will continue, a referring diagnosis is also not important. The overall mapping of the patient's dynamics is important, but this is just the beginning and no hasty conclusions must be drawn. The therapist is ready to obtain information about the patient in all of the categories that Eissler and colleagues (1977) and Kernberg (1984) suggest: ego strengths and weaknesses, conflicts and the core conflict, the reality situation of the patient, and beginning genetic information. However, all of this information, along with the subsequent inferences that might be drawn from it, can be worked out at a comfortable pace; it does not have to be accomplished in the first session. This pace, demonstrated by the therapist in the first session, provides an important experience for the patient, who needs to feel that there is no pressure to complete some informational questionnaire, whether written or in the therapist's head. No doubt the patient's anxiety and personality characteristics will evidence some sort of urgency or demandingness, but this must be distinct from the therapist's demands. A further experience the analytic therapist might hope to convey is that talking is a way of working out meanings. Many start therapy with a fear that only final conclusions are worthy of expression. They remain quiet until the idea is worked out inside and only then report it. The therapist wants to establish an atmosphere in which free association is valuable and tolerated as a way of discovering meaning.

Most important is the patient's response to the therapist and *Relating* the therapist's response to the patient. An initial sense of this can be obtained in the first session, with the therapist observing it from the earliest contact. The therapist needs to observe and register the patient's resistance to interventions and then the patient's responsiveness to interpretations about that resistance. I suggest the term *micro-assessment* because each action of the patient, each omission, each negotiation between patient and therapist, each question or complaint is part of the communication and part of the assessment. No aspect of the first session is unimportant to the assessment of who this patient is. These minute interactions are the content of the patient's transference and the therapist's countertransference. Rothstein (1990) helps us look closely at these experiences. He discusses the question, common enough among therapists, about whether or not they like the patient and whether this knowledge is useful in the assessment and determination about continuing. Rothstein identifies these experiences as countertransference and thereby makes the experience more discernible. It is the countertransference and the transference that from the first session will constitute the most useful data and become the avenue to assessment of the patient.

Micro-assessment occurs in a trial of psychotherapy. In contrast to Freud's (1913) trial of psychoanalysis, this is actually a more flexible process. The range of patients deemed appropriate for formal psychoanalysis has been broadened. The range of patients treatable by psychoanalytic psychotherapy has always been considered broader than those for formal analysis. With advances in the technique of psychoanalytic psychotherapy and the wider range of therapeutic activities that might be tolerated in psychotherapy, the therapist is right to make a trial of almost any patient who is requesting help. If one screens out those asking for something other than psychotherapy (letters for the court, evaluations, weight-loss programs, and the like), then one can take the stance that most likely psychotherapy will be the recommended treatment and the assessment will proceed to ongoing therapy.

The first session is a beginning, but just a beginning. Everything cannot and must not be done in the first session. That would constitute a comprehensive evaluation ending in some report. A far more circumscribed goal for assessment is presented by the first session of a long-term psychotherapy. The therapist must be free to follow the patient's story and will minimize any pressure to accomplish more than can be done in one meeting. It is an aspect of the analytic stance that whatever is to be accomplished in the treatment will take a reasonable amount of time. The beginning demonstration of this must occur in the first session and in the method of assessment. A therapist's urgency to comprehensively gather information or accomplish too much in the first session sets an attitude that is not consistent with what will occur over the course of treatment. The therapist's urgency will then cloud assessment of the patient's anxieties.

Motivation for Treatment

Freud (1913) directed attention to the patient's motivation, and warned against those seeking treatment at the coercion of others and not because of their own suffering. He expected they would not succeed. Many patients seek treatment ostensibly at the suggestion of others. Those coerced by the courts or ancillary programs will have a hard time using the therapist well, especially if the referring agency requires some progress report. They require a form of therapy that is qualitatively different in most cases from that for patients who seek help personally. The therapist experienced with such cases may be able to locate some source of motivation in the patient and exploit that anxiety or pain for the patient's good, but the beginning resources are severely limited. As it used to be remarked, the secondary gain is too great—that is, release from probation.

But many others appear for therapy pressured by spouses, parents, other family members, friends, or even employers. In these cases the motivation is hidden at best, and the pressure from others will soon wane as a substantial reason for continuing. Contemporary psychotherapists need not be so pessimistic as Freud. The man sent by his spouse or the woman sent by her sister must have felt some inkling of pain, some unconscious connection with the relative's complaint to seek the treatment. It will be the therapist's task, one more difficult than with the person who is self-motivated, to locate that pain. The patient must experience the pain to remain a patient. In the first session for a patient seeking treatment under these conditions it will be necessary to direct the assessment toward the pain.

WHAT WAS IT THAT YOU WERE EXPERIENCING, THAT LED THEM TO SUGGEST THERAPY?

Many individuals come to the therapist well aware of how much they are suffering. While the assessment will proceed to understand the depths of the suffering, the fact of it will not be in question. In the face of a person suffering a great deal, the therapist must strike a careful balance. The resistance to or denial of the pain must not be encouraged since that will only serve to end the motivation for treatment and imply that therapy is a matter of ignoring rather than analyzing.

"Normalizing" — shaming too? You're normal... why can't you cope?

As I listen to therapists these days, I hear more references to the technique of normalizing. This typically refers to explaining to the patient that her fears, anxieties, fantasies, or impulses are like those of any normal person. Such a technique may have some guarded usefulness in the course of therapy, and perhaps we all tend toward some measure of normalizing in a countertransference reaction with patients at times. But in a first session I think such an intervention is not only nonanalytic, but could lead to the demise of the treatment.

Normalizing quite directly attempts to minimize the pain or

anxiety that the patient is expressing. Consider a patient who has managed to arrive at a first session and who has already made a considerable effort against a wide range of defenses that resist the appointment. He may be fearful of judgment, ashamed of some behavior or thought, fearful of being crazy, or even actually crazy. The patient may have harbored this thought for a long time and only now makes the effort to speak about it. He has made a commendable effort to bring this very difficult observation to light, in front of a stranger. The expression is fraught with anxiety and perhaps not fully expressed. Then the therapist says, "That's okay, everyone has that thought."

What is the patient's unconscious experience in the face of this advice? I think his experience may take several possible directions, all with potential to thwart the therapy and hopes of analyzing these experiences. Normalizing directs the patient away from a careful and thorough exploration of the experience and all of the emotions connected to it. This sort of intervention also undermines the patient's self-assessment. It says, "Your anxieties about yourself are silly; no one else in the world has such anxiety as you do about that kind of thought."

The therapist's earliest expression of empathy with the patient occurs around the expressed or unexpressed pain the patient feels. One of the significant experiences for the naive patient in analytic psychotherapy is that another person, finally, without urgency or demand, listens to and tries to understand the pain. The degree to which a therapist is able to convey this in a first session will intensify the patient's motivation to continue. Normalizing that pain, failing to recognize the pain, or aiding the patient in defending against the pain will all serve to lessen the patient's motivation and threaten the continuation of therapy. The patient must feel that the therapist takes his concerns seriously enough to treat them.

Levels of Motivation

A significant assessment of the first session is of the level at which the patient enters psychotherapy. Experienced psychotherapists and psychoanalysts may regularly see veteran patients who are familiar with the process, have already established a sense of motivation, and do not need much assistance in beginning the analytic collaboration. This, of course, must be assessed, and the experience must be distinguished from that of the anxious patient who has limited experience but must defend himself with a display of knowledge.

  The more difficult patient is the one naive to psychotherapy. The therapist must accurately assess the level at which to meet this patient in the first session. The naive patient likely comes to the first session with an expectation that arises out of some other experience. Perhaps appointments with medical doctors are the most likely prior experience, but often by the time such a patient reaches the therapist's office this expectation has already begun to unravel. Consider the many differences. The physician has layers of support staff that insulate her from the first meeting with the patient. A receptionist has made the appointment, the first order of business is insurance billing, and the doctor is often seen running about in the back offices as the patient signs in. The patient is made to wait and the doctor enters, briefly says hello, and embarks on a quest for a diagnosis. Most likely the therapist takes a very different tack, one that immediately conflicts with these expectations of the patient. Differences between the practices of physicians and therapists are probably much greater today than ever before in the way a new patient is met for a first session. These differences heighten the patient's anxiety, and to no particular end—even perhaps at the risk of causing an awkwardness that will hurt the start of therapy. Thus, for a patient assessed as naive, some additional attention to education about the process is in order.

  Patients unfamiliar with therapy do not know that the therapist will probably return their phone call, that the therapist may take calls throughout the day, into the evening, and on weekends. This is part of our attention to patients' needs and to confidentiality. The potential patient is probably unaware that the therapist will likely be willing to discuss in the first phone call some concerns about starting treatment. The patient is likely to find an unstaffed reception room or an unfamiliar and even disorienting signal light, and not know to wait for the therapist.

These become unexpected initial experiences for the naive patient, and a few words of explanation early on will avert some of the iatrogenic effects of our unique ways.

Some therapists rightly call the first session a consultation and make it clear to the patient that the session is designed so that both the patient and the therapist can decide if this relationship seems like it will be useful. But the important part of this is what is going on in the trial. The trial is a time of experience, a time for micro-assessment in all perspectives. The therapist must consider the patient from the most general sense of diagnosis to the most minute aspects of how this patient responds to the therapist's voice, words, and way of conducting therapy. The therapist must consider whether he can put adequate energy into this patient and whether there is room in the schedule for enough sessions to meet the patient's needs. The patient must make a decision about whether to continue with this therapist and whether she feels this treatment will be of value, enough to put time, energy, and money into the project.

SOME FIRST-SESSION SYMPTOMS

Urgency

I am interested in some common patient presentations that confront the therapist in the first session, and I have selected some instances to illustrate important first-session concerns. Many patients come to their first session with great urgency. They state the need for something right now—whether it be drugs, advice, or consolation. The person has waited too long before making the appointment, she has held onto the therapist's card for months thinking that she could make it on her own, and now the anxiety is too great. Or the person has experienced some traumatic event—a spouse has abruptly left, or a loved one has died. Whatever the presenting concern the patient presses urgently for help.

I do not believe that the outpatient psychotherapist is met with truly urgent matters very often. However, the patient feels a sense of urgency and this must be respected with an empathic attunement to the individual facing you. The reality of a person's urgency must be assessed accurately. The suicidal patient, the one threatening imminent action, the psychotic individual experiencing florid symptoms, or the person otherwise presenting a realistic danger must be dealt with in a manner that provides containment beyond that afforded by outpatient psychotherapy. The therapist able to manage dangerous cases often has the necessary hospital privileges and ancillary contacts to provide an adequate level of containment. The necessity for this is often quickly assessed, sometimes in the phone call. The patient who feels urgency, but who is not in danger of taking some action is a different matter.

The therapist must assess the dangerousness of any new patient. This is a requirement of licensing laws and a responsibility of any therapist entering into work with individuals who could be suicidal or violent. However, in many outpatient practices the patients referred are not so imminently dangerous or in a state of emergency; this is more the population of emergency rooms and crisis telephone lines. The patient appearing for psychotherapy, however, may present with an experience of urgency and crisis. Ogden's (1989) patient, cited earlier, came to a session feeling a desperate need to make a telephone call to his wife. Ogden met the felt crisis with an analytic, not an emergency room, response, creating an analytic experience between himself and the patient.

The patient's experience and manner of telling it form the beginnings of the transference presentation. The therapist's reaction will affect the future of treatment. Being able to distinguish between the patient's experience of urgency and real urgency, the kind that requires immediate action on the part of the therapist to contain a patient's dangerous actions, is an important skill. By readying therapists for real dangers, the field of mental health has overstated the frequency of real urgency and the need for therapist action. If therapists could sit still longer and explore clearly this distinction with a new patient there might be fewer emergency room visits, suicide reports, and medication referrals, and a good deal more direct psychotherapy.

Compliance

Many patients come to therapy with the symptom of compliance. They have bent themselves to the overly harsh demands of a demeaning father, they have buckled under the guilt laid on them by a needy mother, or have otherwise mirrored themselves to the narcissism of a parent. These are individuals ready to ferret out the therapist's demands—whether obvious or not—and to accommodate, identify, and again use their familiar ability to get what they need by being a good child. These are also individuals enraged at the losses they have sustained in bending to the other, and who subtly resist, obstruct, and act contrary to any demand put to them. Such patients often seem very easy in a first session. They enact what physicians always seem to be asking for—compliance. A compliant patient follows the doctor's orders, takes the medication, stops smoking, loses weight, and makes another appointment.

In the psychotherapy office, patients who are so compliant are also so hard to get to, so difficult to find in the room, and so frustrating in the conscious and unconscious ways they find to obstruct the therapist's work. The therapist can be made to feel that he is treating some image of himself rather than the person in the other chair. Each negotiation is made harder by the compliant person and this is a clear concern for the first session. For example, the therapist will suggest a meeting on Tuesday at 2:00 P.M. and the patient will readily agree. The patient then mentions under his breath that he does have an appointment with someone else at 1:30 that day. The therapist suggests another time and the patient responds that the 2:00 P.M. time will work fine and that he will rearrange the other appointment. The therapist then gets a phone call Tuesday morning canceling the appointment because of a conflict.

A patient struggling with life in this way will regularly present this symptom over the course of the therapy. But it is especially difficult in the first session because the therapist does not know who she is dealing with and compliant patients often seem agreeable and in control of their lives. Perhaps the early evidence pro-

complicant patient → who are we really
dealing with? what are they / who are
next resp

vided by such patients displays a wish to know exactly what the therapist wants, what questions the therapist has, and so on, as if the patient has no pain or anxiety motivating him to the treatment. Compliance must be recognized early on in the therapy and drawn into the work to avoid obstruction of the therapy by the unconscious resistance.

Therapist Anxiety

Another notable symptom in the first session originates in the therapist, not the patient. Therapists entering the room with a stranger for the first time are also anxious. The therapist has an edge because she has done this more times than the patient, but each of us feels anxiety. One purpose for the therapist's personal therapy is to gain greater understanding of these anxieties and the typical defenses against them. In the first session, defensive actions by the therapist can disrupt the process of setting the stage, and deserve some attention. They result from therapist self-assessments that could well lead to further personal therapy or consultation.

This is not an exhaustive list of therapist responses to anxiety—human dynamics are too complex for that—but we will consider some examples. Perhaps the therapist feels a good degree of first-session anxiety, even some uneasiness about his skills. Uncomfortable with facing the new patient, he gives him history and insurance forms to fill out before beginning the session. But the therapist must meet the patient and begin the therapy—a talk therapy, not a treatment of forms. If the therapist fears to meet these anxieties, how can the patient be expected to enter into the experience?

Therapist anxiety often shows itself in chitchat or social conversation at the first meeting. Ogden (1989) makes a strong point that the therapist does not yet know the patient and does not have any idea what meaning might be applied to these offhand remarks. The analytic therapist must be cognizant of unconscious meaning, and this must be part of all communication. The therapist's social conversation merely serves to suppress anxiety, not a valued activity at the start of therapy.

The therapist in anxiety about the degree of pain the patient is presenting moves in to comfort him, may make rapid "contact" with him, or may otherwise substitute an action for exploration or analysis. These again are nonanalytic interventions and non-analytic beginnings. It is the mistake made by the physician cited by Freud (1910) in the paper "Observations on Wild Psycho-Analysis," who, not knowledgeable about psychoanalysis, made several recommendations of activities to a female patient. Each recommendation was either offensive to her or untenable, given the anxiety she presented. In effect, he directed her away from her pain and away from the careful exploration of the anxiety she presented. Whether from his own anxiety or his lack of knowl-edge, he set the course away from analytic treatment and into the worst of suggestive treatment.

Even therapists make unconscious slips at the start of treat-ment. Perhaps all therapists have forgotten a new patient, addressed a new patient by the wrong name, come late to an appointment, or otherwise revealed some unconscious conflict about beginning with this patient. Perhaps the slip reveals some therapist anxiety stemming from information picked up in the phone call, or maybe it suggests greater ambivalence about taking this patient on at this time. Whatever the conclusion, these are signals for the therapist's self-assessment.

SOME ASSESSMENT CONCERNS AND CONTROVERSIES

Suitability and Analyzability

A great deal has been written about suitability for treatment, which is essentially the question of whether the patient's prog-nosis can be determined in an initial assessment. Freud's (1913) trial of analysis was designed to determine the patient's ability to form a transference. Some patients were deemed unable to do this and thus unable to enter into the transference neurosis of formal analysis. Contemporary psychoanalysts are more inclined to see most persons as able to form a transference; the questions then become, Who will be able to establish a useful working relationship with the therapist around this transference, and who will be able to sustain the rigors of an analysis? Kernberg (1984) represents those who distinguish some patients, such as those with narcissistic and borderline conditions, as unlikely to be able to manage the rigors of formal analysis, though able to form a transference. Boyer (1983) treats many severely disturbed individuals in formal analysis without significant alteration of the analytic boundaries or technique.

Psychoanalytic therapy is seen as usable by a wider range of patients, though the question of suitability is still discussed. This is a controversial area of psychoanalytic research, with proponents holding conflicting positions—from those who feel such first-session assessments are paramount to conducting psychoanalysis, to those who believe it is impossible to make such an assessment, and who argue that in fact the assessment of analyzability cannot occur until termination. Some of the discussion in this area takes on a religious quality, as if to suggest that only the chosen are suitable. Yet it borders on silly to suggest that a person "does not want analysis." People do not fundamentally desire analysis any more than they desire surgery, although each is a technique that aims at the relief of suffering. The determination of analyzability must have another goal. If analysts treated only those who wanted analysis, they would soon be out of business.

One valuable application of suitability for analysis is for the assessment of analysands in treatment with candidates in training to become psychoanalysts. Not only do these individuals spend a great deal of time and money in training, but the loss of a training case months into treatment will significantly affect the progress of the candidate's training. An analyst in this position does well to assess carefully the person who is offered treatment as a training case, since it requires a commitment of a year or more on the part of the therapist and thus of the patient.

But in all practicality this is an unusual circumstance. The question of researching who will do well in a certain form of psychotherapy is of concern to us all in the long run, but is most likely not prominent in day-to-day practice. A patient calls and the psychotherapist or the psychoanalyst begins to assess whether or not this patient will work with this therapist. The length of time and the quality of the work remain to be seen, and for the most part we do not insist on commitments of time or of success; we begin a process of finding out, and we move with the experience as it occurs with this patient. Many psychotherapists trained to conduct formal analyses do see psychotherapy patients. Those who do not wish formal analysis or cannot sustain its rigors may still obtain treatment from these highly skilled therapists.

Rothstein (1990) does not place much emphasis on the assessment of suitability. His comments are directed to trained analysts, but useful to the psychotherapist not qualified to conduct analysis. He notes research that indicates many fully trained analysts treat very few patients in formal analysis. Strongly committed to analysis as a powerful treatment, Rothstein asserts that most patients who come to his office (and presumably to other analysts) will most likely benefit from psychoanalysis. It is then the analyst's job to introduce that treatment, analyze the resistances to the analyst's recommendations, and then use the various countertransference experiences to analyze the beginnings of treatment. This is an empirical approach, much like Freud's trial. Rothstein does not put effort into predetermining the patient who might or might not succeed in treatment. Rather, he makes the offer of analytic treatment to the widest range of patients, thereby avoiding the false negative choice— that is, rejecting for analysis a person who might have used it and benefited, but who did not meet the suitability criteria. The psychotherapist might take the same stance, offering psychotherapy to any patient who appears with a complaint and using the best of analytic psychotherapy technique to treat that person, rather than trying to predetermine if some other treatment is more valuable.

Types of Treatment

There is a notion among mental health professionals that somehow the technique rather than the theory of human development ought to direct the treatment. For example, in a case discussion the question was raised as to whether a case of simple phobia ought to be sent for behavioral treatment. This was presented as an ethical issue for the assessing therapist; presumably some outcome research has shown that simple phobias are best treated in a behavioral model. Perhaps the eclectic therapist, knowledgeable about a wide range of techniques, and using those techniques as tools, would take this approach. But an analytic therapist would see this differently. First, analytic theory immediately brings into question the premise that any phobia is simple; such a diagnosis is not one that arises from analytic theory. Then the analytic therapist might assert that even a simple phobia would be best treated by analytic therapy. Outcome research is fraught with problems, and it is not the therapist's responsibility to be aware of all other known problems and treatments, especially in a case such as this where the expectation appears to be that the analytic therapist fully understands behavioral treatment.

Ignoring Suitability

The rejection of suitability prediction by some therapists is in fact the basis for the advancement of technique in this field. It took the efforts of a number of therapists willing to take on the difficult patient, the untreatable patient, and the lost-cause patient to discover and develop techniques that could address more severe psychopathology. This is how it has come about that psychosis is treated by psychoanalysis today, and that self psychology has become such an important part of contemporary psychoanalysis.

The rules of psychoanalysis and psychotherapy are not rules at all—they are guidelines. These are recommendations that have arisen from the hard work and careful observations of many therapists who have preceded us. Although in training some of these guidelines seem like stale concretizations, they have arisen from the creativity and anxiety of therapists working with patients. Those therapists who were able to understand the guidelines and adjust them to fit a particular patient's unusual presentation found new and useful techniques that resulted in

greater relief for some patients. Breaking the rules has advanced
the theory and technique of psychotherapy. This follows the
pattern set by Freud (1912a), who first saw transference as the
greatest obstacle to treatment and who was, over time, able to
develop the understanding of transference into the greatest tool
of psychoanalysis. Strict adherence to suitability criteria has the
danger not only of keeping some patients from treatment, but
also of inhibiting the creativity of those therapists who are willing
to address unusual patients with the skills they have.

Some Thoughts about Short-term Therapy

Another notion in contemporary mental health practice has it
that the therapist must assess the patient for the most cost- or
time-effective treatment. This concept has no doubt been highly
praised by managed-care firms. With Rothstein (1990), I believe
that psychoanalysis and the long-term dynamic therapies are the
most effective for most patients who seek treatment. Some
would claim that the treating therapist somehow has the responsibility to direct the patient to some "proven" short-term therapy
if that has been shown to be more effective. But most claims of
proven therapy are full of research problems, and have been, even
from the earliest of outcome studies. At the very least the
outcomes are different and noncomparable.

One of Freud's (1913) guidelines protects the therapist from
the criticism of misdirecting the treatment. Freud leaves the
length of treatment up to the patient, allowing only the reasonable indication that shortening it will likely limit its effectiveness.
The analytic therapist might do just this: carry on the psychotherapy, but leave the termination date to the patient. Some
patients will choose to end therapy after eight sessions or six
months or one year, but the choice will be theirs, based upon
experience with the therapist. The therapist may not agree that
all the work is done, but may support strongly the patient's
autonomy in the decision.

Carefully developed short-term therapies are practiced today.
They have a usefulness that does not contradict long-term
psychotherapy; however, the nature of such treatments and the

scope of their usefulness is not the subject of this book. One must bear in mind that these approaches to therapy are different than those of long-term therapy. There is simply no way to compare the two treatments as if they produce the same results. A long-term relationship has a different quality for both the patient and the therapist.

Prognosis and Prediction

Applying our clinical skills to predict a person's future behavior may have a certain guarded usefulness in formal assessment as it is used in the courts, both in criminal and family cases. It may have a usefulness in organizational psychology for determining the value of hiring one or another employee. But in psychoanalytic psychotherapy prediction often limits and restricts our view of a patient and the paths of exploration that might be embarked upon. For example, early in my practice I was referred a man who was described to me by my employer and supervisor as a psychopath who had stolen vast sums of money from his mother that he then squandered on drugs. I was referred the patient in hopes I could work with him, though the sense of hopelessness was clear in my supervisor's presentation, and the expectation, unconsciously conveyed, was that little treatment would ensue. I was energetic to build my practice and naive about the meanings of these diagnoses and predictions. At that time I probably imagined and even expected that anyone could be treated and helped to a high level of functioning. My own assessment of the patient and careful attention to his report indicated many new aspects to the story of his sociopathy. This man continued in treatment, showing evidence of motivation and a deep mourning and depression over the recent death of his father. He continued in treatment many years, struggling with his addictions to a point of recovery, and ultimately managing his mother's financial affairs into a reasonable security for her retirement. He was not a sociopath, and the diagnosis and history I had been given were incomplete if not inaccurate, though given with authority.

This example demonstrates a variety of issues related both to diagnosis and to the diagnosis given in a referral. Quite apart from first-session concerns, a diagnosis of sociopathy is very suspect. I think that truly sociopathic individuals are seldom seen in outpatient treatment. In the above example, had I believed the diagnosis I ought to have rejected the referral out of hand. However, a preferable approach in this and all cases is for the therapist receiving the referral to make his own assessment. First of all, the therapist receiving the referral cannot conduct treatment without a careful assessment. Consider a surgeon urged to perform surgery solely on the basis of the internist's diagnosis and referral; clearly the surgeon will perform a thorough assessment before proceeding. And specifically in psychotherapy, the complex idiosyncratic characteristics that make for a therapeutic fit probably cannot be fully assessed until the therapist and patient begin to work together. Patients with a diagnosis of borderline pathology are cross-referred all the time. Any number of competent therapists will not succeed with the patient, then one will, for intricacies not captured in the broad diagnosis.

The example of the supposed sociopath referred for treatment also illustrates the problem of therapist hopefulness. In that case, the referring therapist should not have attempted to treat the patient because he had already determined the outcome of the treatment: it would not work. In my naive enthusiasm I was not so hopeless and I was able to create a working collaboration with this patient, one that worked for him and lasted for over ten years. Rothstein (1990), a psychoanalyst deeply committed to the process of analysis, encourages the view that such predetermining feelings in the therapist, which often leak into the diagnosis, are most usefully analyzed as countertransference, even in the first session. No doubt in my patient the feelings of hopelessness were projected into the referring therapist and short-circuited a more thorough assessment. A different assessment resulted in a very different diagnosis and the therapeutic outcome which then became possible in this man's work with me. A more useful and perhaps more honest assessment of this patient might have been stated by the referring therapist as, "This will likely be a very difficult case, and I do not wish to treat this man with his presenting problems at this time in my life and my career. If you have the energy and willingness to evaluate this case for yourself then I will refer him to you."

The process of psychoanalytic psychotherapy is one of exploring and evolving many areas of a person's life as well as the experience of a two-person relationship. This is a process of discovery and seems little enhanced by a therapist's clever abilities to predict the next step. Predicting human behavior is fraught with difficulty and controversy. The most prominent area in which prediction would be desirable (and where it is constantly sought) is criminal behavior. Society wishes that psychology could provide reliable indicators of future violent and dangerous behavior in order to inform the actions of judges, juries, parole boards, and custody hearings. Even were a reliable method of prediction available in psychology, its use would be severely limited by a person's rights in a free society. But the basic concern here is the value and even the possibility of prediction in the work of psychotherapy. The research into suitability for psychoanalysis is at the same time an attempt to make a prediction. The careful, though brief, assessment of a patient's characteristics and internal dynamics is made in the hope of preventing a failed effort in psychoanalysis. The fact that some analysts have worked successfully with patients who do not fit the commonly held diagnostic criteria for analysis is evidence of the wide range of human possibility and presentation, as well as of the subjective considerations of patient–therapist fit and the functional capabilities of some individuals despite all one's diagnostic categories.

Prediction as a Limitation

The detrimental aspect of prediction in psychotherapy lies in its possible limitation of the exploration of the patient's experience. No diagnostic category even begins to reveal the many varieties of human experience, much less the endless possibilities of what a patient may present and may be capable of accomplishing. Freud (1913) refers to this as the plasticity of all mental processes. If prediction prevents a therapist from allowing for the possibility of exploration of some aspect of the person's inner life, or prevents the expectation and encouragement of some growth, it has limited the possibilities of the therapy. The importance of what I am calling micro-assessment lies in its preservation of these possibilities. In this most detailed assessment, the therapist is interested in how the patient responds to this particular situation—the therapy experience with this therapist—and all of the transference and resistances stirred in this situation. Analytic therapies have always maintained a close focus on this degree of detail. While there is useful and necessary generalization to broader characteristics of the person's functioning and dynamics it is only in the analytic situation that the many rich details of this person's life can come to light.

My concern about prediction and prognosis is to assess how these activities are useful to the beginning of a psychotherapy. The skill of making an accurate prognostic statement or an accurate prediction from psychometric data has value in many areas of mental health work. Research that will better our predictive abilities in areas of violence, or with individuals at risk for certain unacceptable behaviors may greatly aid our society in getting help to those in need before it is too late. But with regard to psychotherapy, our efforts to predict may prevent the successful use of psychotherapy by one who does not present the right constellation of characteristics. The list of variables that must be accounted for to make an accurate prediction about the success of psychotherapy between an analytic therapist and any given patient is simply too immense.

Exploration of Firsts

Some of the literature that deals with first-session issues and presentations does not fall so easily into the category of suitability assessment or technical recommendations. There may be no indication of an intention on the part of the therapist to determine whether or not analysis will proceed. Rather, the writer is investigating first events, or perhaps is enthusiastic about a unique presentation of a patient. These events may not be universal and are not intended for prediction, and the writers do not even seem concerned about any wide application; they are simply presenting events with a certain patient worthy of detailed description.

Beratis (1984) offers us an example. He analyzes the first dream of a patient. The work described in his paper takes as its starting point a variety of other papers that have used the first dream as predictive of analyzability or of the course of the treatment, although some of the research he cites actually failed to produce any predictive information. Beratis takes this one instance and considers the first dream from a retrospective standpoint. The dream did mirror the process that ensued. Beratis does not seem to apply this single example as a general rule, but he does have enthusiasm for this first experience with this particular patient. Much of the work of psychoanalytic therapy is exactly like this, a unique experience between two individuals in an analytic collaboration.

This exploration of first-session issues is a demonstration of the best of analytic beginnings. Each patient makes a unique presentation of himself to a particular therapist. The therapist's stance is one of readiness for the way this new patient presents. Even though the symptoms and dynamics can be categorized, the events at the beginning of a long relationship allow the therapist to recognize and appreciate the uniqueness of this person and the uniqueness of the therapist's own response to him. This is the basis of an analytic collaboration, or an analytic dyad, or a therapeutic alliance, one in which two persons meet in a unique way to discover meaning.

Chapter 6

Transition to the Opening Phase

As we complete the arrangement of the fee, it seems to me that Gregg will most likely want to continue in therapy. In my characteristic manner I ask, "Gregg, do you want to make another appointment?" He hesitates for a moment and says, "Yes, sure, that's what I came here for." I respond, "You hesitated for a moment there—perhaps you felt some reservation about my invitation?" I wonder to myself if he hoped somehow to avoid the therapy, or if I might say, "Everyone feels that way, there's nothing wrong with you." I don't say those things, I hope that I've communicated an empathy for how deeply troubled he felt and that therapy might be an avenue to feeling differently. I wonder too if the fee was startling to him. Gregg responds, "I didn't really know what to expect. I guess I hoped this would be more simple and now I want the session to go longer. But now I'm worried about how I'm going to pay for it, and that it might take more time than I figured." He pauses, thinking to himself. Since we're a little bit over time, I say, "Gregg, perhaps you'd like to think about all that's happened today before we make any specific arrangements about continuing. Since we're out of time for today, may I suggest that we meet again—maybe this week—and continue what we've started?" As I open my appointment book and Gregg reaches for his and begins to open his checkbook, I reflect on how mundane this activity of making schedules and writing checks seems in contrast to the earlier part of this session. Gregg and I may be starting a profoundly intimate relationship that will influence each of our lives in yet unknown ways.

TRANSITION—WILL WE MEET AGAIN?

I have repeatedly made the point that the first session is no more or less psychotherapy than any later session, that one must start psychotherapy in the very manner in which it will continue in the future. On the other hand, at any point in the therapy what is occurring is different in some ways from what went on before. In the middle phase the rhythm of the work together is established and many details of the dynamics between patient and therapist are known and being worked with and worked through. In the termination phase the many themes and experiences of the therapy are being consolidated in preparation for parting. Clearly, the first session differs from all other sessions in that patient and therapist are unknown to each other and the very first experiences together are being assessed by both. The opening phase is distinct from the first session in several important ways, for reasons I am presenting here. In the first session, only the most initial assessments are being made and a contract is not yet solidified. In the opening phase a contract to continue in treatment has been established, even if only a tentative agreement to continue for a short or unknown period of time. But the fee is set, some schedule has been arranged, and the initial experiences of how therapist and patient are going to speak together have been arranged. In the opening phase, questions about whether or not to continue are placed in the background, or at least when they arise a greater understanding of the resistance involved in such questions is known. In the first session, the question of whether or not to continue has a more realistic aspect, as both patient and therapist are faced with a question that might more possibly end in a decision to act, that is, to stop the enterprise before it begins. In the opening phase and later phases the possibility of terminating takes on a different aspect and may be viewed in terms of resistance, acting out, or at times become a more thoroughly assessed decision that patient and therapist do not fit.

Deciding on a Second Session

The first issue of transition to the opening phase is whether or not to have a second session. This may be an overlooked question for the therapist, as often enough we are expecting the patient who consults for a first session to continue, just as we often expect that the patient is somehow aware that treatment may take considerable time. But that may only be the therapist's idea and not in the mind of the new or especially the naive patient. Thus such issues, like all matters of therapy, must be handled directly and clearly, possibly engendering an exploration of what the patient expects, realistically or not. I ask specifically if the person wishes to come for another appointment. I believe that several issues and meanings are at work here. First, many naive patients are not aware of how therapy might proceed and how long it might take. Most of the cases referred to me will require some period of time for the patient to have a subjective experience of change, and even more time to effect what I might consider lasting change. The fantasy of the patient must be considered here. The patient seeking a quick change in her presenting problem may even believe that one session, or just a few, will solve all the problems. Unfortunately this notion is even more common today in the age of managed care. I have seen brochures advertising seminars offering training in the treatment of patients by a few or even one session, and even one that was called "short-term treatment for the long-term patient." These notions have come into the awareness and expectations of the public. I imagine that more patients will be seeking psycho-therapy with some expectation, now more concrete, that therapy will only take a very short time. It is the analytically oriented psychotherapist's task to help the patient become aware of the extent of therapy that will be required to meet the expected changes that she seeks in their consultation. If the person expects to be cured quickly, a simple offer of another time may begin to reveal this fantasy. For example a man I saw in a first session spoke as if he intended to continue for some time. He had come at the encouragement of his spouse, who had been in an extended therapy, and the problems he presented surely required more than the forty-five minutes he spoke to me. He had some long-standing job difficulties that he noted were similar to problems in other areas of his life. At my question of whether he would like to meet again, he replied, "Well, things seem to be getting better already." It seemed that he only reluctantly set a second session. I felt sure that some resistance to therapy was at work here, and he later canceled the next appointment and never returned. The issues of the amount of contact and length of treatment were never adequately addressed.

Consider a first date. Both parties contemplating a first date no doubt have fantasies of where that date will lead, whether this person will be the one to continue with into a long-term relationship or even marriage. Except with the most youthful of daters, fantasies of the future and permanence are inevitable. But that is not a topic of conversation for the first date. In fact some would imagine that the slightest hint of something long-term (much less marriage) on a first date would likely make it a short-lived event. The first date is too full of unknowns for all but the most cautious assessments, too full of anxiety for all but the most superficial of first exchanges. Only the impulsive or those naive to the complexity of human emotions would believe that a first date could reveal everything about the other person. For a first date the goal cannot be a commitment; the only goal of a first date is to get through the evening in a comfortable enough way. Then the only planning from there will be whether or not to have another date, just one more, a second date to build upon the first. There is no need, except perhaps for the most desperate, to consider a vacation together in the summer, a weekend away, living together, or meeting her mother. The first date need only lead to a second date. Then maybe both parties will have sufficient information to make a bit of an indefinite agreement to continue for a while.

So with the first session. Most of all, the first session ought to lead to consideration of a second session. Even though the therapist may feel ready for a commitment to long-term treatment and even though the patient may feel "I don't want to have to go through this again," the only realistic conclusion to just forty-five minutes or an hour together is to consider doing it again. The patient who is in crisis will not be so concerned with the fit; that patient will initially need a competent therapist who can make and follow through on appropriate assessment decisions. For him, the decisions about long-term treatment and the assessment of the therapist will have to wait until the crisis is sufficiently settled to allow for clearer thinking.

I have often suggested to people who ask about how to select a therapist that in many ways one session is far too little time to make such a serious decision. It is more reasonable to make the decision about whether to continue after three or four or even twenty sessions. It is more reasonable, but probably less practical and less often the way we make our decisions, serious as they are.

The Pressure to Act

A feature I have noticed with many patients I have seen is the tendency to attempt to solve their life problems through action rather than self-reflection. We are a society of quick solutions and action-oriented cures. People wear T-shirts stating the philosophy "Just Do It" as a balm against fear and anxiety. The early task with individuals of this sort is to slow the action, to allow for the experience of self-reflection to begin to have an effect, and to allow the emergence of the fantasy and motivation behind the action. To be sure, these actions, perhaps including acting out, are the individual's means of adapting. Ultimately, as they are observed in the course of treatment, these actions become the gateway to understanding the unconscious. But in the beginning of treatment, such tendencies to action may include the demise of the treatment. The early phase of therapy for such individuals will be a careful, thoughtful attitude of reflection about the actions that the patient presents, with the goal of providing enough tolerance of anxiety to go on with the analytic work.

Another aspect of slowing the process of action is recognizing the patient's tendency to jump to conclusions. One person I worked with would regularly respond to an intervention with the comment, "So that means I'm doing such and such, I see that, I'll stop." The response I had hoped for was some furthering of the associations around the issue we were exploring at the time. Her comment suggested a rapid finish to the exploration and directed us away from it. She drew a too-early conclusion to my way of thinking and made further analysis of that issue impossible at that time. Therapists do this as well, often in the rapid labeling of some symptom and concluding with a name for the symptom rather than an extended examination of the anxiety and the depths of that anxiety. Especially in the early stages of treatment I would hope to avoid such conclusions if only for the purposes of demonstrating to the patient that the work of therapy is an extended process in which any conclusion is open to further consideration. In the first and early sessions quick conclusions can suggest that there is no depth to be discovered.

The most important feature of the transition to the opening phase of treatment is setting another session. As focused as this study has been on the first session, it is nonetheless one of many similar sessions. Everything that must happen there will also continue to occur in later sessions. Yet all the matters I have discussed as essential to the first session cannot occur in one forty-five minute period; the process of this first session must flow into the next and the next. I try to set the next session within a day or two of the first, demonstrating the value I place on frequency of meetings. If it is clear that the patient will only be coming once per week or that we can set a regular schedule during the first session, then I proceed with that agreement. But often the second session is scheduled before any agreement about frequency or regular time slots can be determined. So the second session is a continuation and further development of what has happened in the first.

Chapter 7

The Phone Call

The first session is not the first contact with the patient. In contemporary practice the phone call is typically the first contact. The therapist has listened to the patient's voice and manner of requesting a return phone call, most commonly through the use of voice mail. The patient has gotten some clues about the therapist from the sound of the therapist's voice on the phone and the nature of the voice mail announcement. While this process is less personal than it was in earlier days, when the therapist or a receptionist answered the phone, our potential patients are as familiar as we are with electronic communication and some advantages for early assessments may be found in this technology.

Voice mail makes some of the tasks of early communication a bit easier for both parties. Some answering services of the past garbled messages and moreover could not promise confidentiality, since a person had to receive the call. Such systems did not allow for any extended message from the caller, and the therapist had no initial sense of the caller's voice, mood, urgency, or capability of communicating a clear message about his needs. The therapist picking up a private voice mail has some initial information about the patient even before returning the person's call.

Similarly, the person calling for an appointment has the opportunity to listen to the therapist's voice and then take a moment to explain his wishes for a return call. Since many potential, but naive, patients may not expect this convenience, they are not ready to make full use of it. The caller also has an opportunity to assess the therapist too harshly, so therapists do well to consider the tone and quality of their announcements. While all of this is not the most important part of starting therapy, it is a factor, and is a potential place for misunderstandings at a time when the parties know nothing of each other.

When I call back to speak with the patient, I prefer it if the person can get to the point—make an appointment and discuss the concerns for therapy then. Every therapist welcomes such readiness in a patient. But most phone calls do not go that way. If the therapist has an unending list of new callers she may be very selective, but most therapists are in a place to take new patients and each call is worthy of one's best effort to engage the person in a first-session meeting.

The phone call, regardless of how brief, may be considered a shorter first session in which all of the above-discussed issues of stance, contract, and assessment come into play. A contract is begun by simply negotiating a meeting time for the first session. This is a precursor to all of the negotiations of contract that will occur in the first meeting. An assessment must also be made. First, the therapist must determine if the patient is requesting a service that he provides. This can often be quickly addressed on the phone. A more difficult matter is assessing the issue of urgency. The therapist must be able to meet the patient's needs within a reasonable time frame. If the therapist cannot set an appointment within a day or so for the deeply distressed patient, that patient probably should be referred. If the therapist is leaving for vacation at the end of the week, taking on a new patient is probably not prudent, since the therapist does not know how much attention that patient will require. These matters must be assessed on the phone. Ideally, I hope to spend a brief period of time on the phone, enough to establish an appointment, determine that the patient is appropriate in a broad sense, and convey to the potential patient that I am focused on her concerns and that they are best handled in a face-to-face meeting. I try to make that appointment within a day of the call.

The phone call is the very first contact with the patient. It is a time when all of the possibilites for missteps and miscommunications—and their effects—are most intense. It is a limited time during which the ability of the therapist to convey understanding and sensitivity to the potential patient may make for a successful entry to a first session. All of this is possible, no matter in what surprising way the patient may make contact on the phone.

Chapter 8

My
First
Session
with a
Patient

My method of beginning treatment has evolved over the years. I have talked to supervisors and colleagues, listened to patients, and spoken with colleagues who have been patients of other therapists. Much as we all do, I have gathered information about this complicated and complex process called psychotherapy, and the early chapters here have demonstrated my way of conducting a first session. In this chapter I will give an explicit description of what I do when I first meet a patient. For the purpose of describing my first session I have identified eight tasks I hope to accomplish in the first session. Then I describe how I go about accomplishing those tasks.

1: Atmosphere of Safety—Stance

Foremost in my mind for the first and all following sessions is the importance of establishing an atmosphere of safety. I believe that psychotherapy can only proceed if this feeling of safety and holding is available to the patient, and constantly restored when it appears to have been lost. There are many complexities to the feeling of safety for the patient that are conveyed both verbally and nonverbally. Some of the nonverbal aspects of safety rest in the arrangement of the psychotherapeutic space. For the first session, the literal arrangement of one's office may enhance or detract from the experience of safety. Most important, however, is the experience conveyed to the patient by the therapist's stance, an attitude that places safety as a high priority.

2: Patient's Presentation—Assessment, Micro-Assessment

I want to get a sense of the person and how he responds to me and to a new and unfamiliar situation. I watch the way this person expresses and contains his anxiety and other affects. I monitor the changes this person makes over the course of the session to observe how he responds to the various interventions I make.

3: History and Present Circumstances—Assessment

I want to know the immediate and recent past circumstances that have precipitated this person's initiation of therapy. I want and need to know this person's weaknesses, but I also want to know his strengths, one of which is evident in the act of arranging for therapy. I want to begin to get an overall picture of the person, a kind of global map, the details of which will be filled in over a significant period of time if treatment continues. I listen to how this person tells me about his family and development or if he dismisses that history as unimportant.

4: The Possibilities of Therapy—Assessment and Transition

I want to convey to this person that something can happen in therapy. I do not mean by this a sales presentation or educative talk. Hopelessness is a great deterrent to therapy and an unconscious or even conscious expectation many patients bring to their treatment. Sometimes it is the therapist who brings the hopelessness to treatment and this too must be acknowledged and assessed. In some cases I am not hopeful for the patient and I may not be the best therapist for him.

5: Assessment of Myself—Therapist Self-Assessment

I want to assess my own willingness and ability to treat this person, and to see whether my reactions and responses show that we are both capable of making contact. For example, if I have great difficulty understanding the person's way of speaking or have trouble conveying a sense of empathy with the person, I may not be able to treat him. A colleague may be better suited to this treatment. In some cases I have neither the willingness nor the energy at a particular time to treat the patient, perhaps due to anticipating some particular demands a very deprived person might make on me as a therapist.

6: Set Fees and Schedule—Contract

I want to establish a contract that covers both the practicalities and the nature of working together in an analytic experience. In each aspect of this negotiation I emphasize a spirit in which I respect the patient's needs and wishes. I also want to demonstrate that I respect my own needs and wishes and that I will try not to violate those of the patient or myself in the process of negotiation. In the first session, certain practical matters must be arranged, at least the setting of a fee and the arrangement of a time to meet. This is usually accomplished, but if the patient's distress is great these matters may be left to another session. I do this in an effort to convey that the patient's needs have a special priority and that his needs and wishes will be the foremost guide to our work together.

7: Is This for Me?—The Patient's Assessment of the Therapist

I want the patient to get a sense of me, how I respond to his words, how I listen, how it is to sit with me, and even what can be gathered about me from my appearance and the arrangement of my office. This is necessary if the person is to be able to make some kind of assessment of me and of the desirability of working with me.

8: Next Steps—Transition

I offer to arrange a second session if it appears that we will be continuing together. I try to offer a time that is attentive to the patient's urgency, sometimes the next day or even the same day if the person's distress warrants it. This does not necessarily establish the contract for ongoing treatment since the initial assessment may continue for several sessions.

These are the broad goals I have for a first session. I demonstrate in my stance that further time may be necessary to accomplish these goals. In actuality, the substance of these goals is usually accomplished in the first session. Like any experienced therapist, I have a pattern I generally follow in a first session that is intended to accomplish the above goals. I try to stay as flexible as possible with this pattern since each patient is unique and presents in a new and sometimes unusual or unexpected manner. I am ready to change my approach dramatically if the patient's needs necessitate it.

STEPS I TAKE TO ACCOMPLISH
THE EIGHT TASKS OF THE FIRST SESSION

The following are the actions I take to accomplish the tasks described above.

I go to my waiting room at the agreed-upon time and hope to see a person waiting for me. My waiting room is private so I have little chance of meeting the wrong person. Shared waiting rooms require a different entry. I extend my hand and say, "I'm Peter Armstrong." I wait for the person to introduce herself and I listen, expecting to hear how this person would like to be addressed. I then say "Please come in," and I gesture to my office and say "Have a seat in the chair or on the couch—whichever looks comfortable." Some therapists prefer to let the patient find her way into the room and locate a suitable chair. Occasionally someone has taken my chair and this has led to an awkward moment as I move the person to another chair. I prefer to avoid this awkwardness in the first moments of our meeting by indicating which chair is mine. After we are seated I say, "We will meet for forty-five minutes. I will let you go ahead with what is on your mind." If the person has come late I say that we will meet until such and such a time, the time the session would normally have ended, and at some point I raise the issue of the person's lateness.

Some therapists begin without any words, leaving the patient to find her way through the unstructured setting and lending much information to the initial assessment. I say what I say in order to set what I consider a minimal structure so that the same assessment can go on but the patient is not placed in an unduly unusual setting. Structure is already evident in the time limit and my statement that I am ready to listen to the person's thoughts. This conveys a sense of safety, in that the person is not left to entirely direct the process, there are clear limits, and I indicate I will take responsibility for matters that concern me. In addition, I think this shows my interest in what the patient is thinking about and that the focus of attention will be on the person's thinking, not on my concerns. I have chosen my first words very carefully. I say, "I will let you go ahead with what is on your mind" for specific reasons. First, the attention is to the patient's thoughts. Second, I do not wish to direct the patient to speak about any particular topic, even problems or symptoms. I hope to prevent from the outset a feeling that I will direct the topic of any session, now or in the future. I simply direct the person to his thoughts, which in subsequent sessions will be the focus of our attention. This also leaves open the possibility that the person may begin to free associate from the outset. He may be thinking at that moment about his anxieties entering the room, or his frustration in trying to find a parking space. I may be able to see immediately some ability of this person to speak of feelings in the moment. I also do not specify that the person talk. Of course the person will have to talk if I am to be of any help. Psychotherapy is a treatment of words. But any patient has a right to be quiet, to collect his thoughts, and to manage his anxiety, and some do this better with silence. Most people do talk, and I consider this fortunate, but I want to make as few statements as possible that direct the person at this stage.

Now I wait. Some people begin immediately stating their troubles and reasons for seeking treatment. This is good and helpful. Others take time to look around the room and perhaps make some friendly comment. This is often a way of making the setting safe for oneself before embarking on what may feel unsafe. I am able to begin to gather the information I need, especially an observation of this person's way of doing things and managing a new and unfamiliar experience.

Not all patients know they are supposed to let me have my words before they begin to speak in some way. For example, I once met with a middle-aged professional man for a first session. As we entered the room, before I could say a word, he blurted out, "What's on your mind today?" This was intended as a joke, but his delivery was abrupt and full of anxiety, and his attempt was to suppress that anxiety. The comment jarred me as it was intended to, but it was an unusual approach to a serious situation. Clearly this man was choking on his anxiety about starting psychotherapy and he had many reasons to push me away and make me feel defensive.

Most patients begin to speak in the first session and have a great deal to say, making it easy for the therapist to listen without having to take action. This is valuable because it is unclear at this point how the patient will experience my activities. The lull often comes in subsequent sessions. I try to intervene as little as possible, allowing this freedom. If necessary I say just enough to get the person going again. I am ready to deal directly and quickly with the very anxious patient or the patient who is in severe distress. I give time to see what will happen, but I do not allow a person to falter so long as to overwhelm him with anxiety. This could create an unsafe situation.

For the person who is extremely anxious I move to contain that anxiety, usually by speaking to indicate my awareness that he is feeling overwhelmed by anxiety and demonstrating that I will act to establish a sense of safety for the patient, even with respect to his inner experience. For example, the patient described above spoke the way he did out of terrible anxiety that was later discovered to be a fear of speaking to a male in authority and then exploding with rage. Of course the depths and intricacies of these feelings could only be dealt with over time. For the first session with this very anxious man, my primary purpose was to make the entry to treatment possible by making the environment as safe as I could and by addressing his anxiety so that his inner environment would not simply mobilize his usual defenses of isolation and hopelessness. I recognized that this man would require me to talk more than I usually might, and that we would have to begin to lay the groundwork for the future, which might then allow for less therapist involvement and more associative freedom by the patient. I knew that with someone so anxious this would take time.

As the patient speaks in the first session I listen to begin to get an assessment of this person. More generally I listen for this person's history, though I do not ask questions to obtain certain information. I listen to try to understand the nature of her complaint and what recent events might have precipitated the consultation. I have in mind a question about how long she has tolerated her anxiety, has she waited until a crisis has emerged, is she hopeful about getting help. I try to ask few questions about these issues; I wait to see what I hear and what I will need to find out in time. Some things cannot be spoken of for a long time. If this person has a great deal to say and does not look to me for assistance, I listen and try to begin to formulate my assessment from the material she offers. Some patients need more assistance, which can range from an empathic recognition of their anxiety to actual suggestions about how to begin. All of these actions provide material for my assessment of what this person can stand and how much I need to do in order for an atmosphere of safety to develop.

Sometime during the patient's presentation I do speak. I want this person to hear me and get a feel for how I will be in future sessions as our relationship develops. I do not want the person to get an incorrect idea that I will never speak, nor do I want to give the impression that I have all of the answers or that I can respond with my ideas before I have heard a good deal from the person. But I want her to hear my voice and some of the ways I say things

in a session. I make some comments that are clarifying or
empathic. This provides a stimulus from which to observe how
this person responds to me and the things I say. I watch to see if
my comment is accepted and adds to the person's presentation,
or if it is felt to be disorienting, or if is taken compliantly, as if my
words were more important than hers. There are two other
comments I try to make that also have assessment value. I try to
say something positive that identifies this person's strengths. I do
this to convey that I believe there is a hopefulness in endeavoring
to work on the problems the person has presented, and that
possibly this strength will be one of the tools that can be used
to build upon. I am also interested in assessing this person's
recognition of her own strengths and her level of hopefulness or
hopelessness. This gives me some assessment of this person's
superego, of how harsh and critical it is. I make a tentative
interpretation in the first session. I do not make some "deep"
interpretation—which I believe is never indicated. Interpretations at any time in the treatment must meet the surface, in the
sense of finding some place of readiness in the patient. Obviously
in a first session this may be a very simple observation based on
the limited information I have at the time. I do this to assess this
person's responsiveness to my way of working and to an analytic
experience.

During the course of the person's presentation I ask if she has
any questions for me. I do this to encourage an open expression
of concerns and thoughts. I can assess this person's sense of
limits, appropriateness, and freedom to interact with me. If the
person asks something I am not inclined to answer because I feel
it to be intrusive, I am given further information and a chance to
begin to negotiate the boundaries of the therapeutic space. Often
this is the point at which the patient asks about fees and whether
I will agree to treatment.

Near the end of the session I say, "Perhaps we could take a few
minutes to handle business matters." Of course this may have
already happened if the patient has asked questions about my fee
or frequency of sessions. But many people become engrossed in
their initial story and if that occurs I take the initiative. If a
patient is in significant distress or seems to need all of the

first-session time to speak to me I will put these matters off to another session, hoping to convey that the person's anxieties and distress will take precedence over my concerns.

The arrangement of fees is difficult for both patient and therapist. I usually state my regular fee, sometimes with an appropriate reduction that I often give to students or other patients who I know ahead of time cannot afford my regular fee. I watch and listen to the person's response. The easiest responses are to those individuals who can afford my fee and so indicate and to those who, for whatever reason, show a visible or audible reaction to the fee. Then I know that the issue of affording therapy must be explored. I am most concerned about the compliant patient who agrees to the fee and presents a good act as to his ability to afford it. When I see or surmise the person's trouble about the fee I invite the patient's exploration of the feeling and the realities. I am willing to take this as far as necessary to establish an agreeable arrangement. I try to talk about the anxieties and the actual circumstances of the person as much as the person is willing to. If necessary and if my circumstances permit it I will lower my fee, at least until the patient's financial situation changes. I try to engender a spirit of negotiation and make an effort to find a suitable arrangement without one of us overpowering the other. If necessary I will suggest a referral to another therapist or to a clinic where a lower fee is possible. I want to convey the possibility of talking about this to a point of agreement. I try not to rush, and if the patient becomes impatient with the time it takes I note that this has to do with his needs and I try to further discover his anxieties about discussing money. Sometimes the patient simply feels that he will be rushed to a decision that is not suitable—in other words, be overpowered by me. But I do not let the patient overpower me either. Sometimes this is done by playing on my sympathies with desperation and need. If I cannot honestly treat this person at a fee he feels he can afford I am doing a disservice to both of us, and if we attempt therapy it will likely end in trouble and conflict. While I may see such a person for several sessions at a reduced rate to solidify a crisis, I will then refer him to an appropriate therapist if the divergence between fee needs and resources is too great.

Once the fee is set and agreed upon I ask only that the person pay at the beginning of each session. I do this for a variety of reasons and I am open to changing this arrangement if necessary. But as I begin with a person I do not know, it seems prudent to see how things go with payment before a whole month or other period of billing goes by. I make it clear if necessary that this is my thinking, and that as we get to know each other better this arrangement may change. It is one of the few requests I make of the new patient. This may also be a time when anxieties and fantasies may be explored, as so much is stimulated by issues of fee and the various needs of therapist and patient. I try to address other needs or requests as they arise in our relationship, in particular the issue of cancellation. My preference is to address cancellation when it occurs. Contemporary policies require some statement of cancellation policy in the written contract, so I have begun to indicate that I expect the patient to be responsible for payment for missed sessions or sessions canceled without enough notice. I would prefer to deal with cancellations when they arise, but licensing board policies are changing our practices. If the patient asks what enough notice is, I let this be an invitation to exploring a need and negotiating an agreement. I do not have a set time in mind.

The next question is whether or not to schedule a second session. I never assume that a second session is going to be scheduled and I ask if the person would like to set another appointment. If this seems strange to the person I indicate that I believe the decision to begin therapy is an important one and that both of us need to think carefully about proceeding. While I treat early patient sessions as consultative, that is, I do not accept someone into treatment over the phone, I find the decision to continue into ongoing treatment is seldom articulated explicitly. It usually evolves over time as a mutual agreement. The more difficult decision that must sometimes be made explicit is the decision not to continue. I allow the patient full freedom to make her own decisions in this matter, which is one of the reasons I ask if she wants to set a second appointment. It is much more difficult for me to indicate that I will not treat. If this decision touches on questions of my fee, the patient may be more agreeable to a referral. While there may be a feeling of rejection, it is more obvious that the patient has a decision here that depends on her own resources. If I decide not to treat because of some request the patient makes, such as hospital treatment or court requirements, the mutuality must be made clearer. I do not wish to engage in a treatment that requires certain things of me. I try to convey to the patient that what she wants is fine, but that it is not something I do. Sometimes this might be that I do not wish to engage in what I imagine will be a very difficult psychotherapy with a patient with intense needs who will require more of me than I feel able to give at that time. For example, patients who are struggling with addictions (and whom I do not categorically see as unsuited for psychoanalytic psychotherapy) often require a kind of extra energy as they work out the addiction and the underlying problems. I do not always feel I have that extra energy, perhaps at times when I may already be treating similar patients.

Finally, current policies have forced therapists to begin with a variety of documents and paperwork, as I have already noted. I leave these matters to the end of the first session. By the time the patient and I have discussed fees and the schedule, most of the concerns of the contract have been stated. I introduce the paperwork and note the matters of confidentiality, limits, and other disclosures. I emphasize that these matters are covered in my forms, and that any question the patient has, or any change desired in that contract can be dealt with in future sessions. I do not want the written contract to imply that there is no room for negotiation.

If I have judged correctly, the session is over by the time all of these matters have been discussed, and we have arranged a second session. I try to stop on time. Often the time runs over a bit, but I try to demonstrate that I will protect my boundaries and limits. This will occur again and again over the course of the therapy, and possibly raise important aspects of this person's dynamics and needs, but it must begin in the first session.

Chapter 9

Special Cases

Therapists in practice wonder what the next person will present, and no doubt their fantasies run to the perfect patient. That person may be relatively naive to treatment, but highly motivated because he feels significant anxiety. He can describe those feelings and has enough knowledge about psychotherapy, perhaps from a friend, to know that it will take some time and that probably one or two sessions a week will be necessary. He is a hard-working professional and earns sufficient income to afford the therapist's regular fee. It might be a stretch, but it will be workable. The patient can come during his lunch hour, or sometime near the lunch hour. There is no history of mental illness in the family and the patient functions independently. Few patients appear just like this and most appear with more challenging presentations. Some typical ways patients do appear for psychotherapy are considered below. Therapists need not wait until the perfect patient arrives, but can derive benefit from all the unique ways by which people come to seek psychotherapy.

THE PATIENT WITH PREVIOUS THERAPY

Many patients are not naive to therapy. Today, in contrast to the situation in Freud's day, we provide therapy in an age of mental health; even the media encourage individuals to seek treatment, and modalities of therapy abound. Many patients who seek therapy are doing so for the second or third time. However, this does not change the therapist's first-session stance, or even the issues that must be handled in the first session. The fee must still be arranged, assessments must be made, and the analytic therapist must still recognize the meanings of first-session actions and words. But the patient is not naive and comes with another set of expectations and even habits from the previous therapy. A careful ear to assessment will likely reveal these expectations. When a patient has been in therapy previously, that will become a factor in the current therapy. The patient may expect the new therapist to be just like the old one and a complaint may develop around this point. Or the patient may want a very different therapist because of some experience of hurt that was probably evidence of transference. By understanding the patient's hurt, the new therapist may be better prepared to manage the transference in the new therapy. For example, a patient who had been in once-per-week therapy for a period of years transferred to a more frequent treatment with me. She was a very timid and fearful woman and slow to voice any complaint or irritation. It became apparent that her previous therapist would characteristically allow the session to run beyond the set time. I believe that this was done out of a grave concern for this very disturbed patient. I was punctual in the beginning and ending of sessions, and after a period of time the patient made note of this. While it felt like a reduction in the session time she had come to expect, there was also a relief, since she had come to fear that she owed more to the therapist because of the additional time. Working through this experience with me gave rise to various new feelings and transference reactions.

There is reason to be cautious about the patient's reports about the previous therapist. Patients—and for that matter any individual, in therapy or not—report events with a wide range of distortion. Sometimes this is intentional and conscious, sometimes not. The analytic therapist is cognizant that what the patient reports to the new therapist is full of nuances that are best understood in terms of transference and resistance. A report about the previous therapist's failings or even successes must be taken in that context. In the negative report, the patient may be seeking to win the therapist's support and collusion in judging the previous therapist's work. This often serves to deflect negative transference for a time, but the unwary therapist can later be caught off guard when he is in the previous therapist's shoes. In the worst instances of this, a therapist may become party to a patient's legal actions against the previous therapist without any collaborating information. If the therapist is listening for evidence of transference in all that the patient presents, there is a lessened danger of taking the patient's report as truth. Then the therapist can be most helpful in addressing the patient's "truth" and the meanings it contains.

THE RETURNING PATIENT

A related situation is that of the patient who returns to therapy with the same therapist following a hiatus in the treatment. This is a patient who is not naive and furthermore is not naive to this therapist. In contrast to the situation described above, when this patient tells of the therapist's wrongs, the therapist knows the distortions firsthand. One difficulty with a returning patient is that habits have already developed both for patient and therapist, thus screening unconscious behaviors that may continue to go unnoticed. Some breaks in treatment are planned, and the reasons for them—and the potential difficulties they evoke—are probably clearer and have perhaps been analyzed. But many patients break off treatment abruptly, or for reasons that are experienced as a kind of emergency, such as financial problems, and the break has not been so well explored because of the limited time before the break. Sometimes the break occurs in an angry reaction arising out of some transference–countertransference impasse.

I am always moved by the return of a patient. It signifies to me that what we had done together was experienced as valuable. In the case of an angry departure, I feel that the patient's return is a kind of second chance for me and I am grateful, especially if the person's angry departure caused me to rethink and discover some countertransference reaction that could be raised into my consciousness. I feel better prepared to meet the patient and begin to unravel what went wrong. One patient helped me with this as she left abruptly, in one of several partings over our years of work together. She said, as she left the session, "I won't slam the door—which is to say I'm leaving in a way so that I can return."

When a patient returns, his first session is unlike other first sessions; the therapist has foreknowledge, and actually potentially great foreknowledge, of the patient. It is not an instance of strangers meeting, though many other aspects of the first session may apply. The patient has given the therapist another chance to understand differently, or has returned to make further use of the history they have together. What is different from other first sessions is that the therapist must take into consideration matters that might have been missed in the previous contact.

THE PATIENT STILL IN THERAPY

Patients in psychotherapy seek second opinions. The patient may not be aware that that is his purpose, but the consulting therapist must be. When a patient seeks treatment while still seeing another therapist the situation is complex and requires care and consideration. When meeting with such a patient I attempt to conduct the first session in much the way I have been describing, since I want to allow for the possibility of ongoing treatment if that is indicated. But I also try to recognize that this is first and foremost a consultation, even if the patient angrily insists that the therapy with the other therapist is over, never to be repaired. I emphasize that this is a consultation because I think we have all been wounded by the therapist who immediately takes one of our patients into treatment without exploring and evaluating with the patient what the angry or erotic or other transference issue is, in an attempt to heal the original relationship if possible. For all of us, competition and the need to fill our hours can sometimes take precedence over thoughtful and appropriate practice. Perhaps such unconscious or even conscious self-evaluations as "I am the only therapist who can really do the job" come into play here. Therapists have an ethical duty to evaluate these cases carefully and to explore with the patient the nature of the negative transference that has caused the consultation. Of course there are instances where this does not become apparent immediately, either because a patient keeps it secret, or because he is otherwise fearful of discussing the break with another therapist. Here it is crucially important to recognize the nature of the patient's description of the other therapist and the ways in which transference and countertransference may have created an impasse. It does not help any of the parties involved to take the patient's word for it: that is not an analytic exploration.

THE PATIENT IN NEED OF MEDICATION
OR HOSPITALIZATION

Sometimes a patient begins psychotherapy with a request for medication. With a nonmedical psychotherapist, that is a request for referral for a psychiatric consultation. Or another twist is the patient who appears to be in such crisis that the therapist feels an urgency to refer for psychiatric consultation. Many people who come to us for therapy have held onto the referral for many months as their condition deteriorates. They often arrive in a crisis that might have otherwise been averted. Early on in my practice, I remember a young woman who, for a number of months, had been sinking into a depression related to a list of significant losses she was experiencing. She had been referred by her internist, but put off coming to treatment. Finally her husband called because she was unable to stop crying and he was becoming panicky at her condition. Even then they had trouble coming in that day and put the first session off further. This patient was ultimately able to use psychotherapy for an extended period of time and came to therapy three times per week, but a significant effort was initially necessary to deal with the crisis, including hospitalization and medication. Yet other patients come to therapy asking for the referral from the outset, whether or not the therapist feels the need for the consultation.

In cases of crisis or requests for medication, I tend to move more slowly. Of course the assessment in the first session must take place as usual. The therapist must assess the patient's supports, the precipitating factors, and the responsiveness of the patient to the therapist. I try to conduct a first session that could move on to psychotherapy, though I recognize that other referrals and even hospitalization may be necessary, which changes my stance with the patient. This is a crucial issue. The stance of the therapist is changed when referrals are made or when hospitalization is recommended. The therapist must take on more of the role of the expert who directs the patient, and who enters in to take over some significant aspect of the patient's functioning. The therapist is then necessarily allied in the patient's experience and fantasy with the other professionals and their recommendations, treatments, and approaches. I have treated numerous patients in the hospital who have successfully been discharged and who then continued treatment in intensive psychoanalytic psychotherapy. I have also treated many patients who have used medications, either by my referral or because they had started with a psychiatrist before beginning psychotherapy. I believe that psychotherapy can grow out of those experiences, but the therapist must recognize the effect of these other treatments on the therapy. A very different stance is initiated in these other treatments, and the therapist becomes part of those treatments. This position of authority must be analyzed and understood if the move to more traditional psychotherapy is to occur.

In the initial session I try to avert provision of these other treatments if at all possible. If the patient requests medication or is in crisis I try to set a second appointment the next day or even the same day, and I will meet daily to see if some containment of the anxiety can occur or some stabilization can be felt through the influence of starting a therapy and finding a careful listening ear. I expect that the patient who immediately asks for medication has an expectation that psychotherapy will not provide any help or comfort, and that this hopelessness and helplessness, while part of the person's problems, is also a potential deterrent to the therapy. I resist the immediate referral because I do not want to confirm the patient's expectation that therapy will not help. I want to imply that psychotherapy is very powerful and may begin to help with the crisis immediately. Of course in some cases the assessment confirms the urgency and at the first session results in an assessment decision to seek greater containment for the patient. But this need not preclude the initiation of psychotherapy after the person is stabilized in her crisis.

FIRST SESSIONS IN A CLINIC SETTING

Many of my clinical examples, as well as forming the basis of the writing in this book, are rooted in a private practice concept. I typically see patients in my private office and there are no other demands on the first session beyond the needs of the patient and the needs of the therapist. However, many analytically oriented therapists practice in settings other than a private office, and for them certain demands that are not under their control enter into the first session. There, administrative requirements and policies must be attended to by the therapist. I have described what is an ideal setting, in which the patient and therapist are the only two participants in the development of a contract for therapy. Other situations, such as those at a clinic, necessarily involve the policies and administration of that clinic. Presumably, clinics operated by administrators sensitive to psychoanalytic approaches will provide policies that are minimally intrusive and leave the greatest possible freedom for patient and therapist to create the therapeutic situation, but nonetheless policies do exist.

I see two areas of concern. First, the contract for therapy, including setting the fee, policies for cancellation, and informed consent, may all be set by the clinic, with little room for the therapist's prerogative. To argue for the clinic, these policies are often set because clinic therapists move on, especially in internship settings, and the clinic administration must protect its liability in a setting where many professionals of different experience levels are working. Secondly, clinics often have receptionists and standard procedures for intakes and initial session scheduling that circumvent the primary therapist's initial involvement with the potential patient.

Regarding the contractual issues of fee and policies, I suggest that the greatest problems are created by the therapist who feels in conflict with the policies, and who allows that conflict to become a part of the patient's therapy. This can occur in many ways. The therapist may feel that the fee scale is too demanding of his patient and may wish to set fees at a lower rate. A variation on this is the therapist who does not attend to fee negotiation because she receives a salary and has no investment in the income of the clinic. Or the therapist may feel that cancellation policies are too harsh and want to provide the patient with a different arrangement. As discussed in the sections above on the therapist's stance, these conflicts can be felt by the sensitive patient in the transference and will become a factor in the ongoing treatment. I suggest that the clinic therapist who feels such conflicts make an attempt to resolve the issues with the clinic administration by providing the therapeutic rationale for such changes. Again, I believe that analytic therapy is best carried out in a setting that affords the therapist latitude for action with the patient. Perhaps clinic policies may be reviewed with that goal in mind. But even if policies cannot be changed—and often this is the case, since policies are created when groups of people must function together—I suggest that the therapist take ownership of the policy. This will give the best possible foundation to the therapist for addressing the patient in the process of developing the contract for therapy. At the very least one's rationale may be: I practice in the clinic, and since this is the present basis of my livelihood it is my clinic and in my best interests to support its policies in relation to the clinic clientele. The private practice therapist must be cognizant of his limits in terms of fee and scheduling and even in the type of patient he might be able to see at any given time. Similarly, the clinic therapist cannot dismiss these factors of the contract, even if those limits are imposed to some degree by an organization. The therapist who tries to dissociate himself from clinic policies and the effect of these policies on the contract is denying that the patient sees the therapist as part of the clinic system, and that denial enters into the transference.

In clinics, receptionists or intake therapists often take the first call and sometimes conduct the initial session. Obviously, receptionists who are not therapists require specific training in taking therapy phone calls. These preliminary contacts are connected to the treating therapist in the patient's mind. The best strategy is to find some ownership of the clinic process and to remain cognizant of the potential effects it may have on the patient and in the early relationship. Other issues also arise in a clinic setting, such as patient choices about therapists, office sharing, and the need for interns and others to announce their qualifications to the patient. In each case the therapist does well to acknowledge the necessary requirements and conflicts involved in working with others, and to recognize the influence of these factors on the patient beginning treatment. Each concern will be attached to the therapist in some way and begin to point the way to the development of the transference.

THE COMPLIANT PATIENT

I find that one of the most difficult projects is helping the compliant patient to enter psychotherapy. By that I mean helping the patient to move from a position of compliance to one of using the therapy for his own benefit, and being able to find within himself a need for or value for the therapist and the therapy. One might argue that the very disturbed patient or the acting-out patient is more difficult, but these individuals usually present their problems directly and dramatically. While such people challenge the skills of any therapist, their problems and reasons for seeking therapy are evident and immediately available for observation. The compliant patient is not so direct, and often disguises his compliance in intellectual defenses that slow the process of revealing what the therapy is to be directed toward. In the early sessions, compliance can take a variety of forms. I use the masculine pronoun consciously here because I have often treated men who appear for therapy ostensibly at the request of their wives, or, more accurately, at the insistence of a wife who has threatened all manner of consequences if the man does not seek treatment. I believe this is not uncommon, and of course it is not limited to men. Certainly women come to therapy at the request of their husbands and homosexual partners come at the request of their lovers, but in many ways husbands are the most obvious of the compliant patients. Surely all therapists have treated individuals of both genders who are clearly complying with the advice of a referring therapist, physician, attorney, friend, or relative. Understandably, this compliance is a part of the personality structure of the individual, one that often becomes evident when conscious assent to the imagined demands of therapy is followed by passive resistances. Problems with the compliant patient occur when I end up treating what the patient thinks I want to hear rather than what the patient suffers. The most striking difficulty with the compliant patient is that the motivation for therapy is deeply hidden and not just to the patient but to the therapist as well. I suspect that therapy can go on for some time before this is recognized and dealt with in a manner that makes the usefulness of therapy and the motivation for it available to both patient and therapist. Some presentations of compliance I have observed are set out in the following sections.

THE RELUCTANT SPOUSE

A man requested a consultation because his wife, a psychology student, claimed that he had no feelings and never showed her the affection and empathy that she wanted and had discovered to be possible in her study of psychology and her own experience of psychoanalysis. She finally managed to get her husband to consult me upon referral by her analyst. His first presentations were all prefaced by "My wife says that I . . ." This showed rather obvious compliance in his seeking therapy, but there would have been no value to the treatment had the therapy remained focused on his wife's expectations, or his attempts to meet her demands by getting me to direct him to a better compliance with her. Clearly part of his difficulty was that while he was compliant to her demands, he also passively resisted her wishes in many ways because his own experience, conflicts, and motivations were not clearly in his awareness.

THE MEEK PATIENT

A woman who consulted me for psychoanalysis due to long-standing severe obsessive thoughts presented as a very timid, sweet person who would always look to the professional for suggestions as to her next move in life. In fact she sought treatment with me at the suggestion of her psychotherapist of several years because the therapist did not feel that they could meet often enough to effect any suitable change. The patient was very hurt by this suggestion, felt attached to the therapist, and was reluctant to change. It became apparent over the course of therapy that this patient, who ostensibly wanted to know all of my suggestions and recommendations, would not ultimately follow through on the actions she seemingly agreed to. For example, early in treatment she began to use the couch as part of the analysis, at my suggestion. Initially she complied despite some protest, but eventually she sat up and no longer used the couch. It took significant clarification and discussion for her to realize that she experienced great conflict with me over use of the couch and that her action of sitting was more consistent with her feelings. Lying on the couch was only a compliance that could not last, given her misgivings about it. Many similar instances ensued as she often took my comments to be directions about her behavior; she would ultimately resist in her actions despite initial compliance.

THE AGREEMENT TO RESCHEDULE

Another striking evidence of compliance often arises when the therapist or patient must reschedule an appointment. Usually this happens after therapy is in process when a vacation or other conflict arises for patient or therapist that requires rescheduling of a standing appointment. As the therapist offers another time there is a hint that it is not convenient for the patient, but the patient agrees to the time offered. The conflict then becomes evident, consciously if the patient cancels the appointment by phone, or unconsciously when the patient forgets the time. This may of course happen even as the first session is scheduled; however, for a patient who has not yet been seen the possibilities of such a cancellation or forgetting of the first appointment are more extensive.

MANAGED HEALTH CARE

At the time of writing this book, the effect of managed care on the process of psychotherapy and the first session is significant. I thus only repeat what has already been said in many places: managed care in mental health treatment is intrusive, frustrating, and limiting. It has severely eroded confidentiality, and it has placed competent and sincere therapists in difficult positions of liability with patients. Psychotherapists must find solutions to this problem, solutions that do not simply accommodate the system. It is clear that analytically oriented therapists are faced with a growing number of new patients who come insured by a managed-care organization. This deserves attention with regard to the first session.

The contract with such patients is affected in that a third party, one not present in the first session, actually controls significant aspects of the contract that typically are completely within the control of the therapist and the (adult) patient at the beginning of any other therapy. Previously, while insurance companies did intrude on the confidentiality of treatment to the extent that a release of information was signed by the patient, in most cases the insurance company had no further interest beyond the fact of the charges and the need for a diagnosis. Most managed-care companies now set the length of the session, the number of sessions, the frequency of sessions, and the fee. These are only ostensibly set with attention to the needs and wishes of patient and therapist. Furthermore, the contract cannot include confidentiality, since the third party is immediately privy to all aspects of the treatment and, unlike traditional insurance coverage, managed care coverage requires information far beyond diagnosis, dates of service, and charges. The information supplied *by* the patient is then used to limit the patient's access *to* benefits. In addition, the therapist incurs added duties that extend beyond the boundaries of the therapy session, which involve mandatory periodic reporting on the treatment, either by phone or by formal report, requiring energies and attentions to be taken away from the patient. This, of course, influences the assessment. I have discussed assessment primarily in terms of testing and exploring the patient's responsiveness to the therapist, but in the managed-care situation the therapist is required to make a formal diagnosis and description, usually after the first session, thus deflecting attention away from the patient and onto the reporting requirements of the health-care system.

I once called a reviewer after seeing a patient for the first of two sessions in one week, as is common. The patient was sufficiently unclear about the details of his insurance that he did not alert me to call until after the second session. The reviewer asked for a detailed treatment plan. Naive at the time, I said that was not possible as I had only seen the patient two times and felt I was just barely getting to hear about him. She retorted with a finality, "I cannot authorize any treatment with a plan like that, I'm sorry." We were clearly speaking two different languages, except that I was the only one aware of this and she was the one holding the purse strings.

The clinical issues most impacted by a patient's use of managed-care insurance are the loss of confidentiality and the limitation of the length of treatment. With regard to the first session, the therapist who chooses or who must work in a managed-care environment must acknowledge these intrusions to the traditional psychotherapy contract. It will only damage the ongoing relationship for the therapist to deny that these features of the therapy are controlled by the patient's insurer, who is in fact the therapist's employer. But confidentiality is lost not only in the current reporting policies, but also with respect to the patient's insurer, and possibly to his employer. In some instances a patient will be able to recognize this intrusion as detrimental and choose to pay the cost of obtaining treatment personally.

The question of a time limitation must be addressed at the beginning of treatment, so that there is no surprise ending, which can place the patient in a position of loss of the therapy without warning and can also potentially place the therapist in a position of liability. The length of the treatment must be acknowledged at the outset to avoid this surprise.

The broader issues of managed care are not in the scope of this book, but several points bear consideration. I observe that the success of managed care has been obtained at the price of the discouragement of therapists who at one time were ready to enter a long-term relationship with a patient, with all of the excitement and fears entailed in such an endeavor. I think many therapists have been discouraged and dissuaded from that possibility in favor of fixing a patient's problems in the most expedient way, that is to say, getting rid of symptoms, without much involvement in the person's life. In this way many contemporary therapists do not even expect to carry on a long-term treatment.

There also seems to be a feeling that has emerged alongside the growth of managed care that assumes that therapy can only be obtained if payment is made by a third party. It is true that some individuals cannot afford the services of a therapist if they must pay for it out of pocket. But, although not so valued in a managed-care society, therapy is an extremely valuable experience. Perhaps therapists have failed to make the value of therapy more widely known. Worse yet, therapists too have come to believe that therapy must be paid for by a third party. This is not so; many people can pay for therapy, perhaps a reduced fee, out of pocket. But they must, of course, come to value the service. Consider that many people in our society pay for accountants, lawyers, music teachers, sports medicine, plastic surgery, cosmetic dentistry, and personal trainers without third-party reimbursement. Is psychotherapy not at least as valuable as these services?

This is a place for therapist self-assessment. Have we as

therapists become so discouraged about our craft that we assume it cannot be valuable enough to be afforded by many individuals through their sacrifice of some other activity? We must be knowledgeable and skilled therapists to provide a service that people will seek and pay for without outside help. Perhaps part of the first session with the managed-care patient could be an exploration of just how valuable the insurance will be contrasted with the intrusions of the insurer, the loss of control over the therapy, and the attention of a therapist concentrating on managed-care reports.

"Dammit!" Gregg swears as he enters the office and paces toward the window. "How could I have forgotten the session yesterday? I've been doing this with you for what, nine months now?" He chuckles under his breath a bit. His affect was real, though contained by the focus of the work we're doing. He turns to me and says, "You're probably pleased. You love these times when I do something that feels so out of character, so jarring I have to think about what's going on inside of me. And you even get paid for not having to deal with me yesterday." He makes reference to our agreement around missed sessions, one that caused some conflict between us in months past. Gregg sits down and continues. "I can't get it into my mind right now. I can't even imagine missing a Monday session—every Monday, 3:00 P.M. I've been doing this. I just worked right through the time, didn't even think of it until I got home about 7:30. My girlfriend called, we were going to go out to get something to eat. I'd forgotten about that, too, but I was enough ahead of time to cover myself."

"Couldn't cover yourself with me, huh?" I take my opening with Gregg.

"Dammit, yeah. I tried of course. I tried to forget that I had an appointment or missed one. Okay, so what's going on? I'm even forgetting a date with my girlfriend, and I like to see her." He chuckles at his wisecrack about his distaste for psychotherapy. "Oh, I know, we were talking last week about my father. Sometimes I wish I could find a new problem. Seems like I always go back to this stuff with my father. But—forgetting an appointment. You'd think it wouldn't go that way. It's like wasting money to miss the session. My father taught me not to do that. He always worked, you know, worked so much he missed my growing up . . ." Gregg pauses. He caught his association. He is sober for a time. I think I see tears in his eyes. Gregg says, "I wonder what you thought when I missed the appointment. I'm flippantly thinking, he'll just be happy to have the money without having to deal with me. But maybe you did feel something and maybe the fact that I just blew it off, forgot without any feelings, might even make you feel bad."

We go on with the day-to-day analysis of what is happening between us. Gregg and I have created an analytic collaboration evident in his handling of the missed session. Gregg has developed a new relationship outside of the therapy, and whether or not it will last or go further remains to be seen. But meanwhile he and I have entered a phase in which the transference is evident and workable, and we have established a way of working together, a contract that is ingrained in each of us.

References

Anderson, M. (1998). *The pressure to enactment and the hatred of reality*. Unpublished manuscript.

Beratis, S. (1984). First analytic dream: mirror of conflicts and analytic process. *International Journal of Psycho-Analysis* 65 (4):461–470.

Bollas, C., and Sundelson, D. (1995). *The New Informants*. Northvale, NJ: Jason Aronson.

Boyer, L. B. (1983). *The Regressed Patient*. New York: Jason Aronson.

Bruch, H. (1974). *Learning Psychotherapy*. Cambridge, MA: Harvard University Press.

Caudill, O. B. (1977). Documentation: the therapist's shield. In *Therapists at Risk*, ed. L. E. Hedges, R. Hilton, V. M. Hilton, and O. B. Caudill, pp. 263–268. Northvale, NJ: Jason Aronson.

Eissler, K. R. (1974). On some theoretical and technical problems regarding the payment of fees for psychoanalytic treatment. *International Review of Psycho-Analysis*: 1:73:101.

Eissler, R. S., Freud, A., Kris, M., and Solnit, A. (1977). *Psychoanalytic Assessment*. Clinton, MA: Colonial Press.

Ellman, S. (1991). *Freud's Technique Papers*. Northvale, NJ: Jason Aronson.

Freud, S. (1904). On psychotherapy. *Collected Papers* I:249–263.

———(1905). Fragments of an analysis of a case of hysteria. *Collected Papers* III:13–148.

———(1909). Notes upon a case of obsessional neurosis. *Collected Papers* III:296–372.

———(1910). Observations on "wild" psycho-analysis. *Collected Papers* II: 297-304.

———(1912a). The dynamics of transference. *Collected Papers* II:312–322.

———(1912b). Recommendations for physicians on the psycho-analytic method of treatment. *Collected Papers* II:323–333.

———(1913). Further recommendations in the technique of psycho-analysis: on beginning treatment: the question of the first communications: the dynamics of the cure. *Collected Papers* II:342–365.

———(1914a). On the history of the psycho-analytic movement. *Collected Papers* I:287–359.

———(1914b). Further recommendations in the technique of psycho-analysis: recollection, repetition and working through. *Collected Papers* II:366–376.

———(1915). Further recommendations in the technique of psycho-analysis: observations on transference-love. *Collected Papers* II:377–391.

Gitelson, M. (1962). The first phase of psychoanalysis. *International Journal of Psycho-Analysis* 43(4):194–205.

Greenacre, P. (1954). The role of transference: practical considerations in relation to psychoanalytic therapy. *Journal of the American Psychoanalytic Association* 2:671–684.

Greenberg, J. (1964). *I Never Promised You a Rose Garden, a Novel by Hannah Green*. New York: Holt, Rinehart and Winston.

Greenson, R. R. (1967). *The Technique and Practice of Psychoanalysis*. Madison, CT: International Universities Press.

Hedges, L. E. (1999). *Therapists at risk*. Presented at the Oregon Psychological Association, Portland, February.

Hedges, L. E., Hilton, R., Hilton, V., and Caudill, O. B. (1997). *Therapists at Risk*. Northvale, NJ: Jason Aronson.

Horowitz, L. (1990). Psychotherapy as a trial for psychoanalysis. *Psychoanalytic Inquiry* 10:43–66.

Howard, P. K. (1994). *The Death of Common Sense.* New York: Warner.

Jacobs, T. J., and Rothstein, A., eds. (1990). *On Beginning an Analysis.* Madison, CT: International Universities Press.

Kaiser, H. (1965). *Effective Psychotherapy.* New York: Free Press.

Kernberg, O. F. (1984). The structural interview. In *Severe Personality Disorders,* New Haven: Yale University Press.

Langs, R. (1989). *The Technique of Psychoanalytic Psychotherapy,* vol. I. Northvale, NJ: Jason Aronson.

Levine, J. L., Stolz, J. A., and Lacks, P. (1983). Preparing psychotherapy clients: rationale and suggestions. *Professional Psychology: Research and Practice* 14(3):317–323.

Little, M. (1990). *Psychotic Anxieties and Containment.* Northvale, NJ: Jason Aronson.

Meltzer, D. M. (1967). *The Psycho-Analytical Process.* Perthshire, Scotland: Clunie.

Menninger, K. (1958). *Theory of Psychoanalytic Technique.* New York: Basic Books.

Mitchell, S. A. (1998). The analyst's knowledge and authority. *Psychoanalytic Quarterly* 67:1–31.

Ogden, T. (1989). *The Primitive Edge of Experience.* Northvale, NJ: Jason Aronson.

Rothstein, A. (1990). On beginning with a reluctant patient. In *On Beginning an Analysis,* ed. T. J. Jacobs and A. Rothstein, pp. 153–162. Madison, CT: International Universities Press.

Sanville, J. (1991). *The Playground of Psychoanalytic Therapy.* Hillsdale, NJ: Analytic Press.

Schafer, R. (1983). *The Analytic Attitude.* London: Hogarth.

Shor, J. (1992). *Work, Love, Play: Self Repair in the Psychoanalytic Dialogue.* New York: Brunner/Mazel.

Stolorow, R. D., and Atwood, G. E. (1997). Deconstructing the myth of the neutral analyst: an alternative from intersubjective systems theory. *Psychoanalytic Quarterly* 66:431–449.

Strean, H. (1988). *Resolving Resistances in Psychotherapy.* New York: Springer.

Stone, L. (1961). *The Psychoanalytic Situation*. New York: International Universities Press.

Thomä, H., and Kächele, H. (1994). *Psychoanalytic Practice*, vol. I: *Principles*. Northvale, NJ: Jason Aronson.

Winnicott, D. W. (1971). *Playing and Reality*. London: Tavistock.

Index

Abstinence, therapist qualities, 22–23

Acting out, assessment, 134

Ambiguity
first words, 63–64
tolerance of, therapist qualities, 27–29

Analysis of resistance. *See* Resistance analysis

Analytic psychotherapy, defined, 130

Analyzability issue, assessment, 168–170

Anderson, M., 135

Anxiety (of therapist)
first-session symptoms, 167–168
first words, 59–60

Assessment, 125–177
diagnosis, 141–150
Freud on, 146–147
patient–therapist match, 144–146
third parties, 142–144
trial analysis, 147–150
first-session symptoms, 164–168
compliance, 166–167
therapist anxiety, 167–168
urgency, 164–165
first-session tasks, 196–197
law and, 128–129
methods, 138–141
patient history, 140–141
testing, 139–140
micro-assessment, 158–164
levels of motivation, 162–164
normalizing, 161–162
treatment motivation, 160–161
overlooked, 150–158
patient's assessment of therapist, 150–153
patient's self-assessment, 157–158
therapist's self-assessment, 153–157

Assessment (*continued*)
overview, 125–131
prognosis and prediction,
173–177
short-term therapy, 172–173
slowing the action, 136–138
suitability and analyzability
issues, 168–170,
171–172
transference, 127
treatment and, 131–136,
170–171
Attitude
as change agent, 12–15
of therapist, 29
Atwood, G. E., 26
Authority, expertise and, therapist
qualities, 29–32

Beratis, S., 177
Bollas, C., 104, 107, 112, 113
Boyer, L. B., 169
Brief therapy, assessment,
172–173
Bruch, H., 40, 42, 55, 56, 75, 80

Cancellations, fees, 87–89, 90, 91
Caudill, O. B., 105, 106, 108,
109, 111, 115
Change, therapeutic stance,
12–15
Chess, metaphor of, xiii
Clinic setting, special cases,
215–217
Communication, missteps and
miscommunications, thera-
peutic stance, 32–40
Competence, therapist's self-
assessment, 154–155

Compliant patient
first-session symptoms,
166–167
special cases, 217–219
Confidentiality, 99–104
assessment and, 129–131
court orders, 101–103
importance of, 99–100
parents, 103–104
therapeutic stance, 18–20
third parties, 100–101
Contract, 67–81. *See also* Confidentiality; Fees
first-session tasks, 197
fundamental rule, 104–105
length of treatment, 77–80
office setting, 71–73, 96–98
overview, 67–71, 120–121
paperwork, 105–120
ethics, 112–115
generally, 105–106
legal exposure, 107–108
sample forms, 115–120
therapist's notes, 106–107,
108–110
written contracts, 110–112
session frequency, 76–77
session length, 74–76
termination, 80–81
time schedule, 73–74
Countertransference
assessment, 134–135
surgeon model, 23–24
Court orders, confidentiality,
101–103

Dangers, internal, therapeutic
stance, 20
Diagnosis. *See also* Assessment
assessment, 141–150

treatment and, therapeutic
    stance, first session
    technique, 53–54
*Diagnostic and Statistical
    Manual (DSM)*, 141, 142
Directives, first words, 62
Dora case (Freud), 22
Duplicity, therapeutic stance, first
    session technique, 47–48

Eissler, K. R., 86, 143, 144, 158
Ellman, S., 147
Environment. *See* Office setting
Errors, missteps and miscom-
    munications, therapeutic
    stance, 32–40
Ethics
    contract, 112–115
    second opinions, 212–213
    therapist's self-assessment,
        154–155
Expertise, authority and, therapist
    qualities, 29–32

Fees, 86–96
    cancellations, 87–89
    first session, 91–93
    first-session tasks, 197
    generally, 86–87
    policies, 89–91
    reduction of, 95–96
    setting of, 93–95
First session
    assessment symptoms, 164–
        168. *See also* Assessment
    fees, 91–93
    literature on, xi–xii
    pivotal importance of, xi, 4–8
    special cases, 209–224. *See also*
        Special cases
    therapeutic stance, 40–54. *See
        also* Therapeutic stance

topics in, xv
transference, xiii–xiv
transition to treatment,
    181–186
First-session tasks, 195–205
    actions in, 198–205
    assessment, 196–197
    safety, 195–196
    transition to treatment, 198
First words, therapeutic stance,
    57–64. *See also* Therapeutic
    stance
Free association, fundamental
    rule, contract, 104–105
Frequency, of sessions, contract,
    76–77
Freud, S., xiii, 6, 14, 16, 17, 20,
    21, 22, 23, 24, 25, 28, 38,
    48–50, 57, 62, 67, 68, 70,
    71, 74, 75, 77, 89, 93, 104,
    106, 113, 146–147, 148,
    149, 159, 160, 168, 172,
    175
Fromm-Reichmann, F., 41
Fundamental rule, contract,
    104–105

Gitelson, M., 68
Greenacre, P., 16, 17
Greenson, R. R., 24, 87, 95, 97

Hedges, L. E., 108, 111, 115,
    135
Holding environment
    office setting, 98
    therapeutic stance, first session
        technique, 50–51
Horowitz, L., 147
Hospitalization, special cases,
    213–215

Hostility, transference, 16–17
Howard, P. K., 129

Individuation, psychotherapy, xiv
Initial contact, telephone call,
    189–191
Internal dangers, therapeutic
    stance, 20
Intersubjectivity, neutrality, 26

Kächele, H., 59
Kaiser, H., 47–48
Kernberg, O., 53–54, 55, 62, 80,
    84, 133, 143, 144, 158

Langs, R., 68, 97
Law
  assessment and, 128–129
  court orders, confidentiality,
    101–103
  legal exposure, paperwork,
    107–108
  policy intrusions, missteps and
    miscommunications,
    36–39
Length of session, contract,
    74–76
Length of treatment
  contract, 77–80
  psychotherapy, xiv
  short-term therapy, assessment,
    172–173
  therapist qualities, 26–27
Levels of motivation, micro-
    assessment, 162–164
Levine, J. L., 147
Little, M., 50, 51, 75

Managed care
  influence of, xii, xiv

special cases, 220–222
  therapeutic stance, 18
Meaning, search for, 42–45
Medication, special cases,
    213–215
Meek patient, special cases,
    219
Meltzer, D. M., 15, 30
Menninger, K., 68
Micro-assessment. See also
    Assessment described,
    158–164
  first-session tasks, 196
Mirror reference, therapist
    qualities, 24–25
Missteps and miscommunications
  first words, 57–64. See also
    Therapeutic stance
  therapeutic stance, 32–40
Mitchell, S. A., 26, 152
Mother–child metaphor, thera-
    peutic relationship, 17
Motivation
  levels of, micro-assessment,
    162–164
  for treatment, micro-
    assessment, 160–161

Needs, of therapist, first words,
    60–61
Neutrality, therapist qualities,
    25–26
Normalizing, micro-assessment,
    161–162
Notes, of therapist, contract,
    106–107, 108–110

Office setting
  contract, 71–73
  importance of, 96–98
  therapeutic stance, 33–35

Ogden, T., 4, 30, 42–45, 55, 98, 165, 167

Overlooked assessment, 150–158. *See also* Assessment

Paperwork, contract, 105–106. *See also* Contract

Parents
assessment and, 129–130
confidentiality, 103–104

Patient as self-healer example, therapeutic stance, first session technique, 45–47

Patient history
assessment methods, 140–141
first-session tasks, 196

Patient's assessment of therapist, 150–153

Patient's self-assessment
described, 157–158
first-session tasks, 197

Patient–therapist match, assessment, 144–146

Patient with previous therapy, special cases, 209–211

Play, therapeutic stance, 20–21

Policies, fees, 89–91

Policy intrusions, missteps and miscommunications, 36–39

Previous therapy, patient with, special cases, 209–211

Privacy. *See* Confidentiality

Prognosis, assessment and, 173–177

Promises, first words, 61–62

Psychological testing, assessment methods, 139–140

Psychotherapy, definition, 130–131

Rat Man case (Freud), 49–50, 146

Rescheduling agreements, special cases, 219–220

Resistance, first session, xiii–xiv, 5

Resistance analysis, therapeutic stance, first session technique, 51–53

Returning patient, special cases, 211–212

Rothstein, A., 131, 133, 155, 159, 170, 172, 174

Safety
first-session tasks, 195–196
first words, 59
internal dangers and, therapeutic stance, 20
play and, therapeutic stance, 20–21
therapeutic stance, 17–18

Sanville, J., 20, 21, 97, 98

Schafer, R., 4, 16, 17, 23, 24, 25, 26, 27, 28, 29, 55, 72, 135

Schedule
contract, 73–74
first-session tasks, 197
rescheduling agreements, special cases, 219–220

Search for meaning example, therapeutic stance, first session technique, 42–45

Second opinions, special cases, 212–213

Self-assessment
of patient, 157–158, 197
of therapist, 153–157, 197

Self-healing example, therapeutic stance, first session technique, 45–47

Separation, psychotherapy, xiv

Session, length of, contract,
    74–76
Session frequency, contract,
    76–77
Setting of fees, 93–95
Shor, J., 45–47, 55, 56, 151
Short-term therapy, assessment,
    172–173
Silence, therapeutic stance, first
    words demonstrating, 58–59
Speaking, therapeutic stance, first
    words demonstrating, 58–59
Special cases, 209–223
    clinic setting, 215–217
    compliant patient, 217–218
    managed care, 220–223
    medication or hospitalization,
        213–215
    meek patient, 219
    patient with previous therapy,
        209–211
    rescheduling agreements, 219
    returning patient, 211–212
    second opinions, 212–213
    spouses, 218–219
Spouses, special cases, 218–219
Stance of therapist. See
    Therapeutic stance
Stolorow, R. D., 26
Stone, L., 21, 22, 23, 24, 30, 98
Strean, H., 51–53, 55
Suitability issue, assessment,
    168–170
Sundelson, D., 104, 107, 112,
    113
Surgeon model, therapist
    qualities, 23–24

Telephone call, 189–191
Termination, contract, 80–81

Testing, assessment methods,
    139–140
Therapeutic relationship,
    mother–child metaphor, 17
Therapeutic stance, 11–64. See
    also Therapist qualities
    as change attitude, 12–15
    complexities in, 15–21
        confidentiality, 18–20
        internal dangers, 20
        play and, 20–21
        safety, 17–18
        transference, 15–17
    essentials of, 54–57
    first session technique, 40–54
        diagnosis and treatment,
            53–54
        duplicity, 47–48
        holding environment, 50–51
        patient as self-healer
            example, 45–47
        resistance analysis, 51–53
        search for meaning example,
            42–45
        transference neurosis, 48–50
        working together example,
            40–42
    first words demonstrating,
        57–64
        ambiguity, 63–64
        anxiety, of therapist, 59–60
        directives, 62
        promises, 61–62
        speaking or not speaking,
            58–59
        therapist needs, 60–61
    missteps and miscommunica-
        tions, 32–40
    therapist qualities, 21–32

Therapist qualities, 21–32
  abstinence, 22–23
  ambiguity, tolerance of, 27–29
  attitude of therapist, 29
  authority and expertise, 29–32
  generally, 21–22
  length of treatment, 26–27
  mirror reference, 24–25
  neutrality, 25–26
  surgeon model, 23–24
Therapist's anxiety
  first-session symptoms,
    167–168
  first words, 59–60
Therapist's needs, first words,
  60–61
Therapist's notes, contract, 106–
  107, 108–110
Therapist's self-assessment
  described, 153–157
  first-session tasks, 197
Therapist's stance. See
  Therapeutic stance
Third parties
  assessment and, 129–130
  diagnosis, 142–144
Thomä, H., 59

Time schedule, contract, 73–74
Timid patient, special cases,
  219
Transference
  assessment, 127
  defined, 15
  first session, xiii–xiv, 5
  hostility, 16–17
  office setting, 71
  therapeutic stance, 14–15, 16
Transference neurosis, therapeutic
  stance, first session
  technique, 48–50
Transition to treatment, first session, 181–186, 196, 198
Treatment motivation, micro-
  assessment, 160–161
Trial analysis, assessment,
  147–150

Winnicott, D. W., 20, 50–51, 75,
  98, 137
Working together example,
  therapeutic stance, first
  session technique, 40–42
Written contracts, importance of,
  110–112

ABOUT THE AUTHOR

Peter S. Armstrong, Ph.D., is a clinical psychologist and psycho-analyst. He received his training as a psychoanalyst at the Los Angeles Institute and Society for Psychoanalytic Studies. He has been the Director of Psychological Services at Las Encinas Hospital in Pasadena, California, and Clinical Assistant Professor of Psychiatry (Psychology) at the University of Southern California School of Medicine. A director on the Oregon Psychological Association Board of Directors, he is currently on the faculty of the Oregon Psychoanalytic Society and Institute and the Northwest Center for Psychoanalysis. Dr. Armstrong has conduced many first sessions since beginning practice in 1984 and again since moving from Los Angeles to Oregon, where he is in private practice in Portland. This is his first book.

Lightning Source UK Ltd.
Milton Keynes UK
UKOW01n0842150218
317924UK00005B/112/P